WALKING PAPERS

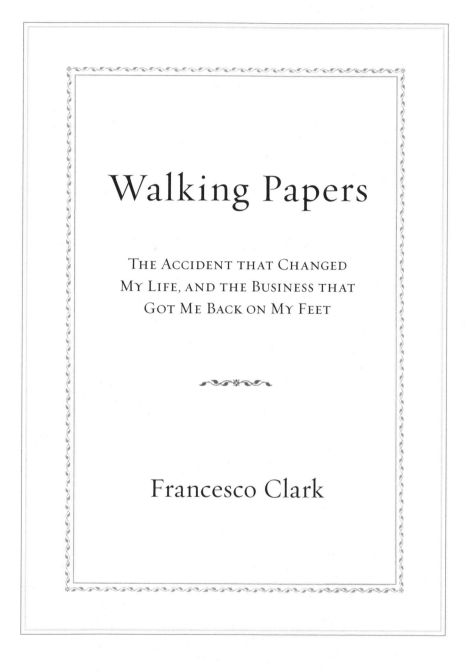

Walking Papers

The Accident that Changed My Life, and the Business that Got Me Back on My Feet

Francesco Clark

HYPERION

NEW YORK

Library of Congress Cataloging-in-Publication Data has been applied for.

ISBN: 978-1-4013-2343-1

Hyperion books are available for special promotions and premiums. For details contact the HarperCollins Special Markets Department in the New York office at 212-207-7528, fax 212-207-7222, or e-mail spsales@ harpercollins.com.

Book design by Karen Minster

FIRST EDITION

10 9 8 7 6 5 4 3 2 1

SUSTAINABLE FORESTRY INITIATIVE

Certified Fiber Sourcing

www.sfiprogram.org

THIS LABEL APPLIES TO TEXT STOCK

We try to produce the most beautiful books possible, and we are also extremely concerned about the impact of our manufacturing process on the forests of the world and the environment as a whole. Accordingly, we've made sure that all of the paper we use has been certified as coming from forests that are managed to ensure the protection of the people and wildlife dependent upon them.

This book, my life, is dedicated to my mother, my father, my grandmother, my sister and her husband, my brother and his wife, and my niece and nephew, whose unconditional love keep me loving life. Also, to Suzan Colon, who taught me how to breathe again and showed me what true friendship really means.

This book is also for anyone who recognizes that you don't need to experience near death to live life to its unlimited potential.

CONTENTS

Part Two

THE NEXT STEP

Part Three

STEPPING OUT

FOREWORD

ALEXANDRA REEVE GIVENS

WHEN MY FATHER WAS INJURED IN 1995, IT FELT LIKE OUR world had been turned upside down. I was eleven at the time, my older brother was fifteen, and my younger brother was two. Our lives changed in an instant, and through the early weeks and months we wondered if things would ever be the same.

Piece by piece, we began to put our world back together again, working to find joy and humor in what seemed like dark moments. My younger brother, Will, celebrated his third birthday in Dad's hospital room with makeshift balloons made from Latex rubber gloves. When Dad got his new power wheelchair, my older brother, Matthew, glued a button on the hand rest with the word "Eject" on it. Letters poured in from friends, known and unknown, around the globe. And in time, Dad began to make progress in rehab and took the first steps to build his foundation for spinal cord research. As so many had done before us, in adversity we rediscovered the building blocks of life: family; friends; humor; faith; and above all, hope.

In the fourteen years since my father's accident, and especially in the past three years that I have served as a director of the

Christopher and Dana Reeve Foundation, I have seen countless families face the same struggles as they deal with the harsh realities of life-changing events. The challenges are many: trying to stay physically strong; navigating the red tape of insurance companies; finding suitable work. Nearly two-thirds of Americans living with paralysis have a household income below $25,000 per year. And yet, time and again, families come together and find reasons to hope.

My father once wrote that hope is like a lighthouse: For it to guide you, it has to be built on solid foundations. In the field of spinal cord injury, countless individuals and organizations are building the foundations for hope, developing new areas of research and promoting programs that help people coping with paralysis to live more active lives. Activity-based therapies are giving some spinal-cord-injured patients significant improvement in their mobility and health. Research into regeneration is progressing, and President Obama's decision to lift the federal restrictions on stem-cell research has opened the door for scientists to explore new possibilities with the benefit of federal funding and oversight. We have a long way to go, but now more than ever, there is much to be hopeful for.

Over the past few years, I have been fortunate to work with Francesco Clark, whose story in so many ways captures the challenges, sorrows, and triumphs of living with a spinal-cord injury. Few people embrace life with as much joy, unity, and infectious good humor as Francesco and his family, and I am honored to call them my friends. Like a lighthouse, I hope Francesco's story will serve as a guide to anyone feeling lost and in need of hope. *Walking Papers* shows all of us that with hope as our foundation, anything is possible.

NOT SO LONG AGO, I BEGAN TO HAVE A RECURRING DREAM. In the dream, I'm floating. My body is weightless, and I'm drifting. I feel completely at ease and at peace, both in body and mind. I'm calm yet self-aware. There are no sounds and I'm without anxiety. I'm bathed in a warm, white light that surrounds me completely. I'm literally floating in the clouds.

My dream is so astonishing that it wakes me up. Instantly, I'm brought down to earth. Back in reality, I don't float and I'm not weightless. I'm made of flesh and bone, and more than many people, I'm subject to the laws of gravity. I have a spinal-cord injury. I cannot feel or move most of my body. Lying in my bed, it's as if there's a giant invisible weight pressing down on me. It is hard for me to turn onto my side, adjust my pillow, or even pull up the sheet unless I have someone to help me. If I'm thirsty and want to drink from the glass of water on the nightstand, I can't reach for it. If I want to get into my wheelchair and leave the room, I have to ask someone to move me. If no one's available to help, I wait.

What does it feel like to be immobilized in this way? After seven years of being injured, I still find this so hard to describe. To put into words what it feels like is like trying to give a blind person an accurate depiction of what it's like to see. It's just so strange. In one sense, I feel the kind of numbness you'd expect after a trip to the dentist, except that my whole body is frozen, from my shoulders down to my toes. Even so, I do still feel *something*. The diagnosis I was given at the time of my injury was that my paralysis was "complete," but in fact, the reality has always been far more complex. Yes, I feel numbness, but it's accompanied by a constant "pins-and-needles" sensation throughout my middle and lower body, the sensory equivalent of static on the radio at a very loud level. Most of the time, this incessant buzzing is just annoying, but at other times, it comforts me—it lets me know I have legs and a body, and that I am alive. I also feel a degree of hot and cold, but in a way that is somewhat delayed. For instance, I can sense temperature in my legs but only after they are very cold or very hot. At times, I feel a sensation of water spraying my skin, like I'm taking a cold shower, but I'm completely dry. I'm aware of pain in my body if it becomes too great, through a wave of extreme heat and sweating. If my left leg is in a lot of pain, the right side of my face will sweat and I feel a surge of heat in my left leg. So, in a sense, I do still feel things, but differently. The signals that my brain receives are confused.

The problem lies at the core of my body, in my damaged spinal column that runs from my brain through the vertebrae of my spine all the way to my tailbone. Until my injury, I hadn't taken the time to think about the essential role that this long bundle of tissue and nerves plays in our everyday lives. The principal function of the spinal cord is as a connector: It carries nerve fibers (also called axons) from the brain to the rest of the body and from the body to the brain. Thanks to the spinal cord, a thousand simple messages are transmitted around the body on a daily basis. The brain wants something, so it asks the body to get it, sending its message through the spinal cord. The body feels discomfort, so it asks the brain to do something about it—again, the message is transmitted via the spinal cord. All this works beautifully, as long as the spinal cord is intact. But when I broke my neck, the two vertebrae just below the back of my head shattered like glass, cutting into my spinal column and severing the connection between brain and body completely. After that, the whole system shut down. The nerve fibers coming from the brain—which are responsible for muscle control and movement—could no longer make their connections. The nerve fibers traveling toward the brain—carrying sensation and vibration—were gone from me. I had become a foreign object even to myself. I couldn't feel, couldn't move. I could still think, but I couldn't do anything about it.

At first, it was my legs that I missed the most—I just wanted to get out of bed and walk. Like most people, I had always taken walking for granted. You wake up in the morning, swing your legs over the edge of the bed, put your feet on the ground, stand up. You begin your day by putting one foot in front of the other. You walk to the kitchen and make yourself a cup of coffee. If you're late for work, you run for the bus. Only when you're unable to get around in this way do you realize the sheer joy of walking: the sound of your shoes slapping on a sidewalk as you leave the house, your arms swinging at your sides, that feeling of going somewhere under your own steam. You don't realize how much pleasure lies in all those tiny imperceptible decisions you make along the way, whether you're going to turn left or right, hop off the curb to cross the street, or whether you're going to stroll or sprint.

These days, it's my hands that I miss more than anything. Nine times out of ten, when I look at my hands and tell my fingers to move, nothing happens. I keep staring. They keep not moving. I stare again. Nothing happens. Sometimes I have to just look away, because if I continue to glare for too long, I feel as if I might go mad. There are so many tasks each day that are off-limits to me without my hands. I can't easily brush my teeth, eat my food, or make a simple phone call. Even scratching my head can be a challenge. I have to think about throwing my arm in the direction of my forehead, hoping that I won't sock myself in the eye in the process. My days are filled with such small conundrums and challenges. How do I reach for a book and open it? How do I turn the pages? How do I switch the light on so I can see the words? How do I get things done when I can't do things for myself?

I miss it all. I want to touch and respond again, to feel texture and impetus, temperature and pressure. Above all, I want to be able to make independent movements. I want to use my brain to command my body. I want to say to myself, "Stand up" and have that happen. I want to think, "I'd like a drink" and then reach for the pitcher and pour. I don't want to live in this way, locked in a body I can't fully control. To me, this is a natural reaction, one that anyone would have in my situation. But even so, the fact that I continue to wish for more is something that many people find challenging. The diagnosis I was given after my injury—and the diagnosis that almost everyone is given after a spinal-cord injury—is that there's no way to get better. "Paralysis after a spinal-cord injury is irreversible," is what I was told. In order for the spinal cord to regenerate, the neurons would need to repair themselves, and this can't happen, apparently. Injured nerve fibers do not regenerate, end of story. Time and again I have been advised to give up hope, to "move on" with my life and "learn to have fun in a wheelchair." But this is easy to say, especially if you're walking around on two feet. Unless you've experienced paralysis personally, it can be hard to imagine what it's like to spend your days immobilized. I often wonder how these experts would feel if they were in my situation. Would they still be so certain that it was best to admit defeat? Or would they dare to hope for more? Wouldn't they want to do whatever it took to get better?

As I write this, it's seven years since my injury and in this time I have become convinced that it is possible to reverse my paralysis. I even have scientific data to prove it. Am I back to where I was physically seven years ago? Nowhere near. Have I improved from where I was at the time of my accident? Absolutely. As I sit here, I can look back over the seven years since my injury and see progression and improvement. Now I want more progression, more improvement. I am determined, but even so, I have my good days and bad days. Every hour I'm awake is filled with a seemingly endless series of obstacles, most of which cannot be overcome without the help of others. But despite this, I continue to try to make the best of my life, mainly because it would make me too sad to do otherwise. My attitude has always been that I am still young and I can only get better. I know I'm fortunate. Although my body was injured, my mind remains my own. I still have a strong sense of myself. I can always go beyond my injury, by sheer force of imagination and will. I can still dream, still be transported, still float in the clouds sometimes.

These days, I know I am lucky. I'm alive. I survived what might have been a fatal injury. This experience continues to affect me in profound ways. I have a newfound sense of the limits of my time on earth. When something like this happens to you, you begin to ask yourself some fundamental questions: What do I want to do today? What can I do differently from yesterday? How should I live? How can I contribute? These are the kind of questions I never thought to ask myself before my injury. Back then, I had no way of knowing what lay ahead on this long path to recovery. I was just going along, growing up, moving forward. I had all the unstoppable energy that comes from being young. I assumed that tomorrow was a matter of course and that it would be pretty much the same as yesterday, except better.

I didn't know that life could change in an instant.

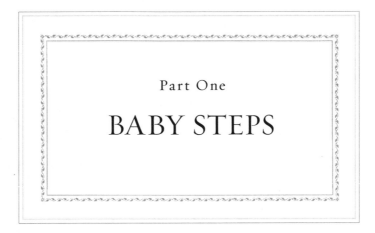

Part One

BABY STEPS

I

~~~❊~~~

Before

MAYBE IT'S BECAUSE OF MY LACK OF MOBILITY SINCE MY injury, but my memories of my younger years come back to me as a blur of constant movement and activity. My mom always said I was a bundle of energy. Even as a baby, I was constantly on the go, determined to keep up with my big brother, Michael, who was seven years older than me. I took my first steps when I was just eleven months old. Even then, I didn't walk; I ran, puffing along behind my brother like a little train.

I was born in February 1978, in New Rochelle, New York, a big, healthy eleven-pound baby with a full head of porcupine hair, the middle child in the closest of Italian American families. I was always vying for attention, always trying follow my big brother's lead. When I was old enough to ride a tricycle, I didn't want to ride a tricycle; my brother had a bike, so I wanted a bike. I wanted to *be* my brother, and if I couldn't be him, then I wanted to be his official sidekick, down to the matching sneakers. When my little sister, Charlotte, was born, I was furious with this small person who had taken my place as the baby in the family, so pinching her whenever possible seemed like the obvious solution.

My mother, smiling, asked me one day if maybe I would like to send Charlotte back? "Sure, why don't we put her in the trash?" I suggested helpfully.

Growing up, our mother was at the center of our universe. We never doubted her complete love for us or her control of our world. I always felt safe if she was there; I never felt that anything could go wrong. She had the knack for making her children feel invincible. In this respect, she was made in the image of her own mother, our grandmother, who lived with us for six months each year. My mother and grandmother are the Italian side of the family. Like a pair of V12 engines, they are the driving force of the Clark household, unstoppable in their energy and affection. My dad has always been the quiet one, the rock, the steady leader. He was born and grew up in New York, where I was raised too, but because my parents were determined that their children would be bilingual, I spent my early childhood going back and forth between New York and my grandmother's home in Italy.

My earliest memories are of my grandmother's apartment in Bologna. I remember chasing after my brother through its maze of rooms, racing our toy cars across the marble floors. In the heat of the summer I would lay on my back in the living room and wait for the tiles to cool me down. At the front of the building, overlooking the street, there was a large terrace that ran the entire length of the apartment. It was filled with wild roses, peonies, geraniums, miniature apple trees in pots. I remember riding my bike down the long terrace, my feet pounding on the pedals, as if the terrace was my raceway and I was overtaking my imaginary competitors. We loved to stay with our grandmother. We devoured her homemade pasta and the cakes she baked fresh for us each morning. Our grandmother knew how to lure us into her kitchen; just by holding out her spoon so we could have a lick of the batter. At the end of the summer we wept when we had to go home.

Back in New York, we were aware that we stood out. Our Italian mother disagreed with many of the activities American parents accepted as a matter of course. She didn't want to send her children to sleep-away camp. She didn't like us to have sleepovers at friends' houses. She didn't want us to wear jeans. We were never allowed to sit around watching cartoons. On weekends, we were marched into Manhattan to visit museums and galleries. Even when we went on vacation there were educational excursions during the day and quizzes and math problems to solve in the evenings. My mother has her PhD in languages; she has high standards and even higher expectations. This could have been intimidating for her children, but instead, her complete belief that we could meet and even surpass her goals convinced us that we'd just have to find a way to keep up.

While our mother supervised our intellectual growth, my father was in charge of our physical well-being. While my school friends were snacking on chips and popsicles, my dad would feed us cashews and dried prunes. My father is a doctor—like his father and grandfather before him—and someone who has always been committed to healthy nutrition. At his family practice, he works alongside my mom, a trained nutritionist and phlebotomist who helps him to run the office, drawing up the nutrition plans and doing the blood work for the patients. At home, my parents were determined that their children should follow the same healthy guidelines they instilled in their patients. Every morning, each child received a cocktail of vitamin pills to swallow. We were served up daily doses of fresh fruits and vegetables. When we asked for soda, we were told we could have ginger-infused, ozonated water. I might have resented it at the time—more than anything, I just wanted to eat junk food like everyone else my age—but now I'm thankful. I don't ever remember being ill as a child.

Luckily, my dad had one exception to his no-sugar, no-refined-carbs rules: my Italian grandmother's cakes and desserts. She defied him to resist them.

"Che tipo di torta vorresti?" What kind of cake would you like today? she would ask us each morning at breakfast. Thanks to my grandmother, my best friends' names are Butter, Sugar, Chocolate, and Bread.

All that food and cake obviously did the trick because by senior year, I was six foot two and a half in my socks. At school I got good grades, but above all, I loved sports—running in particular. I was naturally hyper and needed to let off steam. In college, when I wasn't studying, I was running six miles cross-country every day and I joined the crew team. Although I was never going to make it to the Olympics, it was in college that I learned the athletic mind-set that helped me to stay competitive. I was on a fast track, in all senses of the phrase—pushing myself to go the extra mile in both my studies and beyond. I graduated in the spring of 2000, from Johns Hopkins University, a double major in international relations and romance languages. "Maybe I can be a spy," I'd tell my parents, "then jump out from behind a tree and shout *'Bonjour!'*" When the spy thing didn't happen, I went to work at a consultancy firm in Chicago, moving quickly to *Mademoiselle* magazine in New York, then landing at *Harper's Bazaar.* I was twenty-three years old, a year out of college, and making my way as a fashion assistant at one of the most prestigious fashion magazines in America.

I loved my new life as a graduate. Every morning I left my tiny studio on the east side of Manhattan and walked the sixteen blocks to work on Fifty-third Street. Actually, I didn't so much walk as stride, ducking between the streams of cars and cabs at every intersection, falling in step behind all the hundreds of others on their way to their midtown offices, or scooting ahead of any tourist who dared to stroll. As soon as I stepped through the elevator doors, I headed straight to my desk and my to-do list, where everything required my attention either immediately or five minutes ago. This was not your conventional desk job. I was on my feet all day. I had to get samples back to the fashion houses at a moment's notice; I was forever sprinting down hallways, pushing racks of clothing for the editor in chief's approval. It was my responsibility to make sure every last item of clothing and accessories were ready and waiting when a model arrived for her close-up. I loved the manic excitement of it all, playing my small part in a large team of creative and talented people.

Back then, I was working constantly, often staying in the office until ten at night, almost totally focused on my career. I kept up with my daily running regimen to keep fit, but this was my main activity besides working. I was single and not even dating. I didn't have time for socializing. Often my evenings were spent going to events connected to work. I didn't register that my life was a little one-dimensional, because all my friends were in the same boat. Our focus wasn't on settling down or pairing up. We were trying to become successful in our chosen fields. Like my peers, I kept thinking about what came next. I wanted to be promoted to editor at the magazine, but I knew I was going to have to prove myself first. In the spring of 2002, a year after I started at *Bazaar,* I was approached by one of the big New York public relations firms about coming on board. I knew that working in PR would enable me to understand a different part of the industry and that if I could move back into magazines after that, I would be in a much better position to move up the ladder. And so although I loved my job at *Bazaar,* I handed in my notice, knowing that I had to take this next step. I was running, not to stand still, but to push myself to the next level.

The week before my injury, I went on a short vacation to Florida with my parents and my sister. It was Memorial Day weekend,

2002, and we had booked ourselves a nice hotel on the beach. Every morning, my sister and I went for a run along the beach—I can still remember the feeling of the wet sand beneath my feet propelling me along, the easy warmth of the early sunshine on my face. We had dinner each night looking out over the water, the lights from the marina glittering on the ocean. We toasted each other; we had plenty to celebrate. I was about to begin my new job. My sister, Charlotte, had just graduated from Manhattan College and was starting her master's in biology at NYU in the fall, much to my dad's delight. My parents had worked so hard to put us all through school that their youngest child's graduation was a real milestone for them. They were moving on to a new stage of their lives. My mom and dad—who were in their mid-to-late fifties—talked about retiring soon. Although my brother wasn't with us—he was on vacation with his new wife—we toasted him, too. He had started working in IT, he had moved into a new house. All was well with the world.

I left Florida on Memorial Day Monday, a week before the rest of the family, to return to work. It was my last week at the magazine. That Thursday, my coworkers threw me a little going-away party. We had cupcakes and ice cream. I was sad to be leaving, but excited about the new chapter that was opening up ahead of me. I had that feeling of anticipation that comes from being on the cusp of something new.

The next day, Friday, I took the train from Penn Station out to Long Island for the weekend. A friend of a friend of a friend had put me in contact with a group of people who were renting a beach house for the summer. There were eight or nine other young professionals my age, and they needed one more person to help cover the rental cost, so I leapt at the opportunity. Summers in the city can be stifling, and my shoebox apartment had barely enough room for a bed, a clothing rack, and a kitchenette. At the beach, I would have access to a large house with a yard and a swimming pool, just minutes from the ocean.

The journey to the house took about three hours. When I arrived at the station, I climbed out of the train, swung my bag over my shoulder, and walked the short distance from the station. It was a beautiful, mild evening in May that seemed to hold the promise of the entire summer ahead. I was looking forward to seeing the beach and swimming in the waves the next day. By the time I arrived, most of my new housemates were already there. We made our introductions. Even though I was a stranger in their midst, everyone made me feel instantly welcome, inviting me to join them for dinner at the neighbors'. I accepted. It was getting late, and I was hungry. The dinner had a Mexican theme—Mexican food and nachos were laid out on a big table outside. That evening, I was getting to know people, making small talk, finding out what everyone did, where they lived in the city, and what they had planned for the summer.

After dinner, it was such a nice evening that I decided I wanted to go for a quick dip in the pool before going to bed. By now, it was dark and the pool was dimly lit. Even so, the water looked inviting. I was twenty-four, just starting out. Everything in my life seemed lined up perfectly for the next step. I had no way of knowing what lay ahead. I assumed that the forward motion of my life would continue, because this was all I had ever known.

I dove right in.

2

Breathing, Somehow

THE MOMENT MY CHIN HIT THE BOTTOM OF THE POOL, I understood what had happened. It wasn't the deep end; it was the shallow end. The impact reverberated through my body. I knew I was dying when I realized I was underwater and could not move. My body had shut down. That was it. There was no other explanation; there was nothing else to understand. I was going to die because I couldn't move and I was underwater. My mind was in overdrive. I felt a surge of emotion I could neither hold back nor control. I scolded myself: "Do you know how much physical therapy you will need to do? Do you have any idea?" That was all I could think. I felt cold, but that wasn't important to me. I could only hear my mind screaming beneath this inviting water that somehow had betrayed me.

The upper part of my body floated to the surface, but I couldn't lift my head to gasp for air. I was facedown in the water, my arms suspended in front of me, my knees dragging on the bottom of the pool. I knew I couldn't hold my breath for much longer. I saw small bubbles on the surface, and I began to wonder if these would be the final breaths of my life. Involuntarily, I gasped, my lungs taking in water. I was drowning in four feet of water. I couldn't scream. I couldn't move. I was going to die.

Finally someone realized there was something terribly wrong. I heard a loud splash and my head was pulled up from the water.

"You just saved my life! Call 911!" This was the first thing I said.

"What? You're kidding."

"No. Call 911."

I could taste the chlorine in my lungs, but I couldn't cough out the water. Somehow I was hauled out of the pool. I could feel the wind cooling my wet face very quickly and a surge of blood in my neck, an intense swelling sensation that I thought would suffocate me. I felt nothing else. It was a terrible feeling, not knowing what was happening inside my body. Before the next ten minutes were over, I thought I would die all over again.

Somehow, I kept breathing.

Breathing was all I could manage at this point. I closed my eyes, trying to focus on staying calm, and I opened them only when the paramedics arrived to airlift me to the hospital.

I had never been on a helicopter. I lay on the stretcher, sensing the strong wind forcing the helicopter into the air. The paramedics were talking to me, but I had to keep my eyes closed. All of this was too much for me to handle. I had to prioritize what was most important—survival. Distractions such as talking or being aware of the world around me might be enough to throw me over the edge. I kept my eyes shut for the entire journey and didn't open them again until I was being wheeled into the hospital.

People on all sides of me were pushing and running. A nurse was barraging me with questions. I answered her as best I could. I knew she was only doing her job, but I really just wanted someone to sit there next to me without speaking or moving. I couldn't handle all this activity and noise.

My mind was racing in circles, trying to make sense out of something that it couldn't explain. I smelled chlorine again and started to panic. I felt the liquid in my lungs. I knew this didn't feel like my body anymore. Something was very, very wrong. What the hell had happened to me?

I was taken for X-rays. The doctor came and held the film up in front of me, pointed at the two shattered vertebrae in my spine. I heard his words but couldn't process what they meant. As he spoke, the blood kept swelling in my neck, like a pressure cooker getting ready to burst. All of my pain was focused on my neck and this feeling was so intense that I couldn't fully register that I couldn't feel anything else.

"We're going to have to operate to stabilize and fuse your vertebrae before the swelling causes more damage," the doctor said.

I didn't know what this meant. The nurse rushed over to me to read me some sort of release for surgery. Yes, let me take a look at the paperwork, I told her, even though this seemed like a completely inappropriate time to be dealing with legalities. She held it up in front of my eyes. I couldn't move my arms to pull it close enough to focus. She began to read it out loud. I chose to ignore the clause that said there was a high probability that I might die in the operating theater. Instead, I refocused my attention on trying to make it through the next moment.

My godparents, Therese and Frank, arrived from Westchester, just outside the city. I had given their names to the paramedics. I didn't want anyone to tell my parents yet. My family was still in Florida, due to return home the following day, and I definitely didn't want them to hear this while they were still on vacation. As crazy as it sounds now, I wanted to protect them from the shock of hearing the news. In the meantime, I knew that my godparents would pull through for me. I had known them my whole life and they had come the minute the paramedics had called.

The nurse returned to give us an update: "The surgeon will be fusing your broken vertebrae together to stabilize your spine. Don't worry. He's one of the best in New York."

I whispered to my godparents, "What's she going to say? 'Yeah, the good doctor is on vacation, so we called the other one instead. He isn't all that bad.'"

Looking back, I can't believe I actually cracked a joke in the circumstances, but at the time it seemed like a good way to retain a degree of normality. I needed to break the atmosphere of despair that was gathering all around me. It comforted me to know I still had my mind, when all else appeared to be failing.

I would be going into the operating room within the hour. It was clear that I was going to have to call my parents before the surgery. I gave the nurse the name of the hotel in Florida so that the surgeon could make the call. After he had spoken to them, I would be able to talk with my family. There was a possibility that I wouldn't survive the surgery and this might be my last conversation with them.

In Florida, my mother answered the phone. It was six o'clock in the morning and she had just woken up. For most of the night, she had lain awake, filled with an unidentifiable anxiety without any idea that I had been injured. When the phone rang in the hotel room, she grabbed it immediately. The surgeon asked to speak to Dr. Clark, my father. My mother assumed it was a business call, and told the doctor that Dr. Clark was on vacation and that he didn't want to be disturbed.

"No, I need to speak to Dr. Clark," the surgeon replied. "It's important. It's your son."

My mother's strength left her. She collapsed. She called for my dad.

"You have to speak to this person," she told my father, already distraught. "I can't understand what he's telling me."

My father took the phone. My mother could see from the look on his face that something was very wrong.

My father told my mother, "Francesco had an accident. We have to leave right now. He's having surgery in one hour."

Then the phone was held to my ear so I could speak to my parents.

I could hear my mother's voice. I needed to reassure her.

"I'm here, I'm in the hospital. I'm OK. I can talk to you," I told her.

"You're going to be OK," she said, right away. Even though her voice was breaking, just the sound of her words reassured me. "Don't worry. We're coming."

"I'm sorry, I'm sorry," I told her. I was crying now.

"It's not your fault."

"I'll see you when I get out," I said.

My dad came on the phone. He sounded calm. I took this as a good sign. If he was calm, it meant I was going to be fine. I'd always been fine. He'd always taken care of me.

"Don't worry. We're coming. Charlotte is changing our flights. We'll be there when you wake up."

Charlotte came on the phone.

"Why didn't you call us last night after the accident, Francesco?" my sister asked me. "You can't be so selfless . . ."

I felt like I had failed in everything. I was crying. My sister comforted me:

"It's OK, please don't cry, we're coming."

As soon as Charlotte hung up, she began calling the airline, arranging for the car to the airport, making sure they would be there when I came out of the operation.

As I succumbed to the anesthesia, my parents and my sister were embarking on what felt to them to be the longest journey of their lives. They made it to the airport, boarded the flight, endured the plane ride, were picked up by friends who drove them all the way to Long Island—an interminable drive that took nearly two hours.

When they finally got to the hospital, the surgeon was just coming out of the theater. I had been in surgery for more than seven hours.

My family spoke to my doctor immediately.

"Your son is still unconscious, but he appears to be stabilizing," he told them, matter-of-factly, without preamble. "He's paralyzed from the neck down. He'll never move from his bed. He won't be able to breathe without assistance. I'm afraid he'll have to be on a ventilator for the rest of his life."

My dad is a doctor. He had already understood some of the possible consequences of this kind of injury. But my mother and my sister had no idea the extent of what had happened to me. What the doctor had just said was incomprehensible to them.

"When can we see him?" my mom wanted to know.

"Not long now; he should be coming around soon. Wait here."

"When can we take him home?" my mom continued.

"Hopefully in a few weeks' time. But you're going to have to be prepared. You'll have to modify your house so that he can get around it in a wheelchair."

My mother had just been informed that her son was never going to move again. The last thing on her mind was how to remodel the family home. Let's just say that the steely surgeon did not make a good impression on my discerning mother.

"I just want to see my son," she told him.

Meanwhile, inside the operating room, I was no longer unconscious. A nurse was thrusting a plastic tube into and out of my throat. The pain this caused was so acute, it had woken me up from the anesthesia. Each thrust of the tube was like a knife slicing at my insides.

"I know this hurts," she said. "I need to suction the liquid out of your throat, or you'll choke."

The rawness inside my throat caused by the tube, along with the pressure I felt inside my neck and spine, was too much to bear. I tried to scream, but physically I could not—the intubation muffled even the smallest sound. I had no way of moving and no way of communicating. Finally, the nurse recognized the look of utter panic in my eyes. She stopped and told me to go back to sleep but sleep was impossible. There were plastic tubes and IVs coming out of every part of my body; large machines beeping and buzzing next to my bed. I don't know what else could have been hooked up to my body. This was what I presumed was called life support.

I was still groggy, but awake, being wheeled out of the operating room, tubes and wires attached. This was when I saw my family, waiting for me. I knew I needed to do something to show them that I had survived. I summoned up what energy I could and began thrusting my shoulders forward to say hello.

The doctor ran over too.

"OK, OK," he said, obviously somewhat embarrassed that his prognosis had already been disproved. "But you want to keep the swelling down. You're not supposed to be moving."

I thrust my shoulders again, harder this time.

"Evidently my son disagrees with you, Doctor," said my mother.

3

❧

I Sing, Therefore I Breathe

I REMAINED IN THE INTENSIVE CARE UNIT FOR THE NEXT ten days. I still have nightmares about my time there. The bare room, the metal bed, the sterile smell of the ward, and most of all, the noises. In the next room, I could hear a man repeatedly crying out and pleading to die. These weren't the kind of sounds a person would make in reaction to pain; they were deeper, lower, bestial, impossible to ignore. The nights were the most difficult for me because I would fall asleep early in the evening and wake up at three or four in the morning to the wails of my neighbor. The nurses mostly ignored him. What else could they do? Each time I began to drift into sleep, the moans would startle me back to consciousness, reminding me exactly where I was and what had happened to me.

My life was still in the balance. In the days after the operation, I was tethered to my bed twenty-four hours a day with a tube in my throat, unable to speak. My left lung had collapsed completely in the swimming pool after taking in all that water, which meant that I couldn't breathe without the ventilator tube going in through my throat. This tube—which was hooked up to a machine that inflated and deflated my lungs—was the most difficult aspect of the entire ICU experience. The intense pressure the intubation exerted on my throat caused me to constantly gag and panic. But while I wanted to scream, unlike my neighbor, I couldn't make as much as a moan.

I could think to myself, "I want to move," but I could not move. Every impulse to move remained—to turn or to reach or to sit or to stand—but I couldn't follow through. Besides my ability to just about move my shoulders, my range was nil. The numbness extended from just below my shoulders downward. The rest of my body was gone from me. The only parts I could still feel were the insides of my elbows and armpits where the swelling in my spine had caused certain nerves to become acutely sensitive. Even the touch of a cotton swab would feel like the jab of a pencil. Even three months after leaving the hospital, if one of my physical therapists grabbed me under my armpits, it would feel like a knife was slicing through my skin.

My family was at my bedside constantly. My mom was there every minute of every night; my dad came after his day at his practice; my sister relieved my mom so she could grab a few hours' sleep during the day. They were doing what people do when they're in shock: trying to help while constantly coming up against their own helplessness. They could do little except stay with me, hold my lifeless hand, offer what comfort they could. The only way for me to communicate with them was by blinking or darting my eyes in my sockets. I could clench and unclench my jaw; I could raise my eyebrows; I could shed tears; I could move my eyeballs. And I could blink my eyelids. One blink for yes, two blinks for no. That was it.

I was desperately trying to process what was happening to me. Because I could no longer feel or command my body, I think my subconscious reacted by assuming I had died. Every night, I dreamed I was dying. I dreamed I was drowning. I dreamed I had no legs. I would wake, frantic, unable to scream or move.

I remained like this, on life support, for the next nine days, attached to a tangle of tubes, lines, and wires via every part of my body. I had a feeding tube going up my nose into my stomach. There was a catheter tube going into my bladder. I had two IVs in each arm and another tube that went under my collarbone, dosing me with medication. I had a sensor on my finger that monitored the oxygen levels in my blood, a hard plastic neck brace holding my neck absolutely still, and various sensors attached to my chest and arms, measuring my heart rate. At times I would weep from the shock and fear and helplessness. I couldn't feel or breathe or talk. Any way of connecting with the world was shut down.

There were moments when I didn't understand why I should go on. I knew that I was one breath away from death; only the ventilator was keeping me alive. There were so many tubes coming out of my body, so much electricity involved in my survival, that I barely felt human anymore. The doctors had told me that I was never going to move again. Was I really worth all this effort? What was the point in continuing? Wouldn't it be easier to give up? My family was the only reason I didn't succumb to such thoughts. They were fighting for me. They were doing anything they could to help. My room smelled of the essential oils they were using to massage my arms and legs to keep my circulation flowing. My mom called the Christopher Reeve Foundation and found out that I should be getting methylprednisolone, a steroid that decreases swelling in the spine and increases healing. My dad was on the phone to colleagues in the medical community, finding out about research trials in Israel and across Europe. A doctor in Germany told him, "I'll think about it. I'll come up with something." It was the first glimmer of hope. My mother was calling everyone she knew, telling them to pray for me. I had rabbis, Methodists, Presbyterians, Catholics, Unitarians, all praying for me.

After two days—to my relief—I was told that the intubation tube was going to be removed to see if my body could take over and breathe on its own. My mom and sister were there with me. We were informed that it was likely that I would still have difficulties breathing and would have to be put back on the ventilator right away.

I knew I wanted to do everything in my power to prevent that tube from being put in again. When it was finally out, I inhaled and spoke my first words: "Oh, thank God."

The sound I made was barely a rasp, but at least it was a sound. My throat was raw, swollen, and sore. It hurt to try to swallow, and when I did try to vocalize, only the faintest noise came out. I didn't care. The tube was gone and I was still breathing. It felt so good to actually make some sort of sound, even one that was barely audible; it proved that I was alive. And it gave me a lot of comfort to think that if the doctor was wrong about the ventilator, he was probably wrong about the rest of his prognosis. Soon after this, I began to get a little more sensation back in my arms and shoulders. I was so happy, I cried. I was too weak to move much, but it was a starting point for me, something positive for me to focus on.

That same week, my brother and his wife, Valerie, came back from their trip. They had been on vacation at the time of my accident, on a cruise, and my parents had decided to keep the news from them until they returned. What good would it do for them to know what had happened to me when they were stuck on a boat? When they found out, they came immediately to the hospital. Mike was distraught.

"I should have been here for you," he insisted. "I feel so bad. I didn't know."

Here was my big brother, seven years older than me, usually so calm and in control. I could only imagine what it was like for him and the rest of my family to see me hooked up to all these machines. If it were one of them in the bed, instead of me, I didn't think I would be able to bear it. With the little voice that I had, I told him to forget about it.

"Me being here is not your fault," I said.

"Mike, you're here now," my sister told him. "Let's just focus on getting Francesco better."

This was how we thought about it, right from the beginning: How can Francesco get better? Now that my brother was back, he joined my sister and parents in taking shifts at my bedside. There was always someone there. Every member of my family was helping to connect me to myself, so that I could find the strength to begin the slow fight for recovery. I needed my family most at night. The psychological and physical shock to my body after my injury and operation was so complete that it had carried through to all parts of my conscious and subconscious. My dreams were vivid and terrifying. One night I dreamed I was walking along the sidewalk in Manhattan. It was sunny, cool, and breezy—a perfect kind of late September day. I was walking to work, briskly. In my dream, I was midway to the office, turning the corner onto a side street as the wind blew against my face. But then my legs suddenly began to feel heavy and I struggled to keep my pace. As I looked down, I saw that my feet and legs were turning gray, morphing into the sidewalk, transforming from flesh and blood into stone. The cement began crawling up my body. Soon I was engulfed; it was going to suffocate me. I didn't know what to do. I screamed out for help, but I was completely alone. I couldn't explain what was happening to me—I only knew that I must either escape it or go mad.

When I woke up from the dream, I was yelling, gasping for air. My mother, drowsing in her chair next to my bed, startled.

"I'm here. Don't worry. You're here," she told me, leaning over me, caressing my hair. But I was scared to death. Waking up from a bad dream to find that I was in the ICU was a nightmare come true. Every night I would fall asleep and wake up screaming, relying on my family to restore me to myself. Several times, when I awoke I had to ask whether I had arms or legs. I no longer knew what was real. It was as if my body was continuing to send messages to my brain but these messages were so jumbled and unclear that my brain was reacting by assuming that I'd died.

If nights were bad, the days were not much better. At intervals during the day, a nurse would have to come and suction my lungs. I had lost all ability to use any of the muscles around my ribs. This meant I was physically unable to cough. Because I couldn't cough, I couldn't expel the phlegm and liquid in my lungs, so they would begin to pool in my chest, preventing me from breathing deeply enough for my body to get the necessary oxygen. Whenever my blood oxygen levels fell below a certain number, a godforsaken machine attached to a sensor on my body beeped ferociously and a nurse would rush to my bedside to begin the dreaded suctioning. This involved preparing a foot-long plastic tube and feeding it up my nose, down my throat, and into my lungs. If the tube didn't reach my lungs—which many times it did not, because of my gag reflex—the nurse would have to try it again, sometimes three or four times, until it went in.

"Try to breathe in deeply when the tube reaches the back of your throat. Don't try to swallow, or else the tube will go down toward your stomach instead of into your lungs."

Easier said than done. All I could do was nod as my face turned bright red, my eyes tearing up from the pain. Once the tube was inside my lung, the nurse would turn the suction device on and extract as much liquid as she could through the tube. The most difficult part of this procedure was that I couldn't breathe during the extraction. The suctioning became my most hated activity of the day. By the end of the second day, the roof of my mouth had become so swollen and irritated that even whispering was impossible. I declared war on the blood oxygen machine. I would do anything. I just didn't want it to beep again.

But beep it did. On one particular occasion, a nurse came to suction me but I didn't recognize her. As soon as she inserted the tube, I felt something catch in my throat and I knew this felt wrong. Normally, the suctioning hurt, but this time I was in agony. I turned my head violently to one side, then the other, fighting to free myself. I tried to scream at which point the nurse turned to me and said, "Shut up, stay still, and let me suction your lungs."

So she turned the suction machine on, but the end of the hollow tube was caught in my throat. Looking at the tube, I could see that the liquid inside it was reddening with blood. The nurse grew even more annoyed and pulled the tube out, shaking her head, as if this were my fault. My parents asked that I was never to be treated or seen by that nurse again. I am certain she caught my vocal cord, because after she had finished with me, the little bit of voice that I had was almost completely lost.

Other times, the nurses would perform what they called "Chest P.T." Apparently the P.T. stood for "physical therapy." In practice, this involved wrapping an oxygen mask over a fist to cushion the blow, then hitting my back several times each day to try to loosen the phlegm from my lungs. Even so, it was difficult for me to cough strongly enough to expel anything much. I soon discovered that although I couldn't cough, I could do other things that would help get the phlegm out of my lungs. For instance, I could scream, albeit fairly quietly due to my sore throat. The more I screamed, the more this seemed to clear my passages. But after hearing the man in the neighboring room yell and moan for his life to end, I thought that screaming would be annoying to the nurses and to him. So instead, I sang. I sang horribly and as loudly as I could.

I discovered that not only did my singing help clear my lungs, it passed the time, too. I was in bed, in the same room, without being able to move or leave, not even to go to the bathroom. Television became boring very quickly, and I never cared for the morning shows or soap operas anyway. Reading was nearly impossible, as I was attached to so many tubes and machines, I couldn't move my arms or sit up and keep a book on my lap. Remembering the words and the tunes of my favorite songs became a form of entertainment.

"There's absolutely no way you are going to be able to sit still without doing something, knowing you," my sister pointed out.

And so singing became what I did, although my pitiful little frog voice sounded like a Muppet on helium. Charlotte and my friend Alex, whom I've known since sixth grade, provided me with necessary equipment for my bad karaoke habit: a CD player and a stack of CDs. First up was the soundtrack to *Mamma Mia!* It actually worked quite well; I put the CD on repeat, started singing, and managed to go a full four hours without the oxygen machine beeping. Encouraged by my progress, I decided to keep going. I sang so loud and for so long the nurses actually started requesting their favorite numbers. They would come in and put a CD in the player, and as they would leave, they would just say, "Sing!"

One nurse remarked, "Your poor neighbor. If he wasn't screaming for his life to end last night, I think the sound of your singing might just kill him."

"Well, maybe I can belt out something that will calm him down. A melody?"

"Highly unlikely. Don't put him in a coma on my shift."

That poor man!

But I liked the fact that I had found a way to make the nurses smile. They would stop in to chat for a while, then go back to whatever it is they were doing. This made me feel almost human. I had regained my voice, and people were listening and reacting to me. I was no longer only a body full of tubes, hoping to get better. I *was* getting better, and people would stop into my room, not because I was crying out with pain, but because I was making a fool of myself. I didn't know it at the time, but by singing, by coming up with my own way to clear my lungs, I had taken the first, tiny yet proactive step on the very long road ahead of me.

4

Unhooked

APPARENTLY, THE PROBABILITY OF INJURING YOUR SPINAL cord is even slighter than getting hit by lightning or winning the lottery. I had beaten all the odds. I was a fluke. I had nearly died. But I was alive. I didn't know whether I was the luckiest or unluckiest person in the world. I guessed I was a little of both.

I needed to get out of the ICU. I desperately wanted to be transferred to a rehab hospital. We had heard that the Mount Sinai Medical Center in Manhattan had a department devoted to people recovering from spinal-cord injuries. Here I would be able to do physical therapy. This was the next step. The sooner I left the ICU, the sooner I would feel like I was getting better; that my body no longer needed its robotic appendages to sustain and monitor my lung, heart, and bodily functions. I needed to know what I could do to begin to recover, and I needed to get to that level quickly. But I wouldn't be allowed to leave until I'd shown that I could come off life support completely. I had proven that I could breathe without a ventilator, but I still had a dozen tubes and wires attached to my body. Most urgently, I wanted to show that I could eat on my own so that the feeding tube that went into my stomach through my nose—nourishing my body with a disgusting thick, white liquid which looked a lot like glue—could finally be removed. There was concern that if I was given food or liquid orally, I might choke, because I still had to relearn how to use the muscles in my throat to swallow. I had been deprived of real food for nearly a week now. As a result, I was constantly and incredibly thirsty and hungry.

This was agonizing for me. I had never skipped a meal in my life. Ever. In our family we talk about what's for lunch while we're eating breakfast. When lunchtime comes around, we're already thinking about dinner. When we're eating dinner, we discuss dessert. Somewhere in between meals, we snack. In the ICU, the only real food I was allowed to have was frozen apple juice fed to me on a spoon, just enough to wet my mouth. The nurses were so worried I might choke, they could only give me the tiniest amount to taste. It was torturous. I dreamed of food: chicken, steak, potatoes, pasta—anything edible. The dreams were so real that I could smell and taste each dish, but when I awoke, I was just as hungry as ever.

I was constantly on the lookout for food. One afternoon, my sister came into my hospital room and I immediately asked her if she was eating walnuts or pecans.

"Ummm, no," she replied. But then she thought about it for another moment and said, "Oh wait, yes, I had some nuts about an hour ago."

It turned out that my sister had an open bag of nuts in her closed purse. That, along with her breath, was filling the room with an aroma that made my mouth water. I was so famished that I had become incredibly sensitive to the smell of food.

After about one week of being in the ICU, the hospital sent a speech therapist to test me to see if I was physically able to eat solid food. She brought with her a plastic container with a slice of bread, cheese, pudding, applesauce, juice, and one or two other things inside. It looked like she'd stolen a fifth-grader's lunch box. Even so, my eyes grew wide as she slowly unwrapped some crackers and placed them in my mouth.

"Now, eat slowly. Your throat might be sore. Try to—"

I chewed quickly and swallowed.

"Crackers—done. What's next?"

"Let's try pudding."

"OK. Where is it? What kind?"

"Well, we have . . ." She started rummaging through her box of food.

"Oh, whatever you have is fine. That vanilla one looks great. Feed me."

I ate everything she had in about thirty seconds flat. The speech therapist laughed. She couldn't believe how rapidly I'd passed the tests.

When I asked if she had any more food for me, she laughed again.

"Most people don't ask to eat more hospital food!" she pointed out.

I was already glaring at her.

"I think I can bring more up in a couple of minutes," she said.

That's more like it, I thought. At this point, I would have eaten plain, stale bread and considered it a gourmet treat.

And so the feeding tube was removed. I just had a few IVs and the sensors to go. Every day I would ask when I could be moved to Manhattan to begin my physical therapy regimen. Finally, I was told that it was going to take another ten days. Ten days! This seemed like more than I could bear. Surely there had to be some way to expedite the process. Now that I was off the ventilator and the feeding tube, we started to push even harder to get out of the ICU and into rehab as soon as possible. I was always asking the nurses and doctors for news, updates, advice on how to make my time in the ICU as short as it could be. My impatience paid off; Mount Sinai had an open spot for me. Something to look forward to! Once I got to Mount Sinai, I could focus my energies on whatever the therapists and doctors wanted me to work on, no matter how hard it might seem at first.

"You have to get better," one nurse said to me, the day before I was to leave. What a relief to finally hear some words of encouragement from someone at the hospital. I was longing for that. All I had heard from my doctors in the ICU was "Don't expect to move again." They didn't want to give me false expectations, but even so, I yearned for someone to say "You will get better. I don't know how, or how long it will take, but you will get better." The nurse didn't know me, but she believed that I was strong-willed enough to move forward. She had faith in me. I don't know why or how she saw it, but along with my family, she helped to give me the courage to hope.

~~~~~~

5

Starting Therapy

"WHY DOES THE CLOCK SAY TWO O'CLOCK?" I ASKED MY sister.

"Because it's nearly two o'clock," she told me. "You've slept all day."

My first night at Mount Sinai, my new hospital, I had woken at three in the morning, unable to get back to sleep. A nurse gave me a sleeping pill. After that, I must have fallen into a deep and unshakable sleep, because my sister had been waiting all morning for me to wake up.

I was disappointed and annoyed. Today was supposed to be my first day of physical therapy, and I had slept right through the session. I wouldn't have a chance to go to the gym today. Instead, my therapists paid a visit to my bedside to say hello.

"Hi, my name is Cynthia. I'll be your occupational therapist."

"Hi," I whispered back. My throat still hadn't fully recovered from the intubation. I was thinking: What's an occupational therapist?

"I'll be focusing on helping you to do things through adapting equipment and therapy," she explained. "Things like feeding yourself, brushing your teeth, and what we call ADLs—activities for daily living. . . ."

The way she said this made it sound as if brushing your teeth was the most exciting thing imaginable. Cynthia was upbeat, energetic, encouraging. She was going to help me get better. I liked her immediately.

"And this is Larry, your physical therapist," Cynthia continued, introducing me to her sidekick. "We will be working together with you every day in therapy." Larry seemed like the perfect counterpart to Cynthia. They were both in their twenties, with a routine where one would finish the other's joke, like an old married couple. It certainly seemed as if I was going to be in good hands.

Later on that first day, I had a visit from two of the doctors at Mount Sinai. They had come with good news.

"Francesco, we wanted to let you know that you may be eligible for an experimental surgery that is currently under trial in Belgium," one of them told me. "If it's OK with you, we'd like to see if you qualify. But you would need to get on a plane and go right away. This is only for people who have just been injured."

I didn't hesitate. I told them I wanted to try whatever it was they thought might help me to get better. I was excited to hear about any experimental surgery or research on offer.

It was just such a huge relief to have escaped the ICU. I was in a rehab department now. I was no longer hooked up to machines. I was here to get better, and everyone was going to help me. My expectation was that I was going to recover and I was going to do whatever it took to make that happen. My whole life, I'd been healthy and able and I didn't see why I shouldn't be able to improve with hard work and persistence. I was looking forward to starting therapy the next day.

But my expectations were one thing and my reality was another. The next morning, I got ready to go to the gym. This was a twenty-five-minute process that involved the patient aide getting me dressed, hoisting me into a sitting position, then bracing himself against my torso, so he could haul me from the bed to the chair. This last part was difficult for him and painful for me. The weight of my body pressing against him concentrated pressure on my neck, which was still in a brace.

"Watch your neck!" the aide told me.

"Right," I told him. What I wanted to say was, "Umm, I can't move my body. So maybe *you* could watch my neck."

I hated this helplessness. I hated not being able to do anything for myself. It was humiliating and it was also completely bizarre. But if this was what it took to get me to a gym so I could get to work, then so be it.

Now that I was in the wheelchair, sitting up was harder than I'd expected. I couldn't control my abdominal and back muscles— the muscles necessary for holding myself upright—so my body immediately leaned slightly to one side. I had no way of redressing the balance. I might have been able to move my head in order to shift my weight a little, but the neck brace kept me from utilizing the little mobility that I did have. Sitting up was a little like balancing on a tightrope—except that when I sensed I was about to fall, there was nothing I could do to catch myself.

Cynthia arrived to wheel me to the gym. She helpfully nudged me back into a vertical position and began pushing me down the hospital hallway. People cleared a path so that we could pass. Suddenly I felt like the old guy in the airport cutting to the front of the check-in line. Except I was twenty-four years old.

I was assuming we were going to a gym with lots of equipment, where people would be working out, if only in a limited way. I was expecting a couple of bench presses and a treadmill. I had no idea what we would be doing or how. I thought Cynthia might say something like, "OK. We'll just try jumping jacks, and whatever you can do, you do." I associated the word "gym" with movement and activity. I wasn't prepared for what I was about to see. As Cynthia pushed me into the room, I was met by silence and stillness. Ten or so patients were lying on multiple low wooden tables about fourteen inches off the ground—wheelchair height. Therapists were standing over the patients, stretching their limbs very slowly and gently. One therapist was helping a patient to sit up. Another therapist was crouching down in front of a patient in a wheelchair, awkwardly shifting him onto the mat. For the most part, the patients were just lying there, immobile. Obviously these people were profoundly disabled. Nearly all of them were wearing neck braces. Two of the patients were on ventilators, and I could hear the familiar hiss and suck of the machines. The only people standing up were the therapists.

No one was doing jumping jacks today.

Cynthia remained as upbeat as ever. "OK, so let's get started!"

She began lining up my wheelchair to the wooden edge of the therapy table. This took numerous adjustments. Obviously I had to get from the chair to the mat, but how? I looked down at my legs. Although they still appeared to be attached to my body, they were lifeless, like two pieces of waterlogged wood. I couldn't even begin to imagine how Cynthia was going to get me from point A to point B without the help of a large crane.

"So we're going to do a sitting board transfer," Cynthia said cheerfully. She took out a thin, three-foot-long wooden board. "We're going to use this wooden board and place it under your butt and slide you on it, from the chair to the mat. I'll help guide you by blocking your knees with my knees, and grabbing you at the hips."

I was sizing her up, instinctively, thinking: "Good luck with that. I'm over six feet, and you're about a foot shorter than me."

Cynthia grabbed at my hips and pulled my body forward in the wheelchair. My upper body immediately began to fall in her direction like a giant sandbag. My instinct was to save myself. I willed myself to use my legs, abs, arms, back, anything. But it was useless—Oh God, I was falling! Cynthia caught me just in time; my head was now against her shoulder, her arms still at my hips. It was such an awkward position, with the front of my neck pushing against her shoulder bone, and my butt angled out. The pressure from my entire body pressing up against my neck was excruciating.

"It's OK," Cynthia told me calmly. "See, we just needed to scooch forward in the chair so that your butt will clear the wheel, otherwise you can't slide sideways to the mat."

Rationally, I knew I was going to be all right. Even if I fell, it was only by a distance of about a foot. But even so, sliding off my wheelchair and onto the mat was extremely disquieting. I weighed 190 pounds and I had to trust that this tiny woman would be able to catch me, and that I wouldn't completely crush her in the process. I was still recovering from major surgery. My neck was in a brace and my surgical wounds had yet to fully heal. I was terrified that I might be hurting myself without even knowing it.

"Don't worry," Cynthia said calmly.

Don't worry? Easy for you to say! I just broke my neck after falling four feet and now I can't feel my body! Of course I'm going to worry!

In the middle of my transfer, my butt slipped off the wooden board and I did fall. It was happening so slowly, with Cynthia at my hips, that in fact it wasn't scary at all. I actually started laughing, the whole thing was so ridiculous. Larry rushed over and helped hold me upright from behind.

"Let me kick the wheelchair away with my leg, so I have more room to get him. . . ."

Cynthia was bright red. Her face started to perspire against mine, and she was quiet for the first time that morning. She was holding most of my considerable weight, and she was beginning to shake with the effort.

"I got him, Cynthia," Larry said.

A couple of other therapists rushed over to help, and before I knew it, I was lying on my back on the mat. Cynthia looked as if she had just run a four-mile race. She was sweating, out of breath, and she was as red as a lobster.

"Normally, that's a lot easier to do." She puffed. "How tall are you?!"

"I'm six foot two and a half," I told her.

My height was something that would fool every therapist I ever met. For some reason, I didn't look too heavy to do a transfer, but about halfway through, my long legs would weigh me down, like boat anchors dragging at the bottom of the ocean floor.

"Don't get discouraged," Cynthia told me.

But as I lay there on my mat, I couldn't have felt more useless. This was my first day of therapy, and all I'd managed to do so far was move from my chair to the mat. And I hadn't even been able to do that right.

"It's OK," I tried to whisper, but Cynthia couldn't hear me. On the far side of the therapy room were windows overlooking Madison Avenue. The noise of the traffic was deafening, and I could still only speak in a whisper. Not so long ago, I was one of those people beyond the window, out on the avenue, racing to work, going about their business, contributing to the noise of the city. Now I was on the inside, lying immobile on my back, trying to whisper loudly enough so someone might hear me squeak.

With a shudder, I registered for the first time that I had a spinal-cord injury. Everyone in the room had a spinal-cord injury. I didn't know exactly how everyone had gotten to this point; I just knew that until a few weeks ago, they'd been happily going about their lives just like me. Now they were lying here in this "gym," unable to move as much as a millimeter. Suddenly, being in this place, seeing these people, I realized that from now on I would be defined as "one of them."

That evening, one of the doctors returned to give me an update on the Belgium surgery. I was ineligible. My lung capacity and the severity of my injury meant that the journey and the surgery were going to pose too great a risk. My first few days at Mount Sinai were not going quite as well as I'd hoped.

6

~~~~~~~~~

The New Routine

BEFORE LONG, I STARTED TO GET THE IDEA OF MY NEW routine. I would wake up around seven, at which point an aide would come and get me dressed, which basically involved pulling a fresh T-shirt over my head and wriggling a pair of paper hospital pants over my legs and butt. One of my favorite aides was Diane, because she never stopped talking. She was such a happy soul that her mood was infectious.

Every morning she'd bustle into the room with a barrage of friendly patter—"Oh, you look good today! You slept well, didn't you? Yes, you did! Are you excited for therapy? Yes, you are!"— without ever pausing to let me answer.

The other nurses and patients treated Diane like the den mother, and she was one of the few people I actually trusted to do my wheelchair transfer without causing me a large amount of pain. She was as strong as an ox. She would lock her knees against mine, then she would throw my upper body over her shoulder and quickly drop me down into my chair.

"Done!" she'd say, brushing her palms together.

Then Diane poured me a bowl of cereal and began to feed me

small amounts. I knew this was the only way I could get food inside me, but still, I was a grown adult, sitting here, being fed by a forty-year-old woman. Diane wasn't doing anything wrong, but every time she lifted the spoon to my mouth, it felt like a slap in the face. It was hard to hold myself upright, so I was always leaning off to one side. Every now and again the milk from the cereal would dribble down my chin, making me feel like even more of an idiot. After a while, I would just listen to Diane's chatter, trying to forget what was happening to me. I was hungry, and I had no choice. I simply did not have the arm or hand control necessary for lifting a spoon or a fork to my mouth.

This was one of the biggest adjustments I was going to have to make; from now on, others were going to have to do everything on my behalf. Everything was slower, everything was a production, everything was a big deal. Getting washed was bizarre. A nurse helped me shower, but I had no sense of being touched, so I was completely detached from the experience, registering it only with my eyes. It was like I was wearing armor and someone was wiping down the metal. I couldn't feel and I couldn't help; I could only watch.

When the lights went out at the end of the day, all I could hope was that I would lose myself in sleep for long enough to forget that I was going to have to go through the same routine all over again in the morning.

Apart from visits from my family and friends, the other aspect that helped to relieve the monotony was my weekly group-therapy session. Every week, about ten patients from the rehab ward would gather in the common room to meet with a social worker or a psychiatrist. My first time, I had no idea what to expect. I guessed this was probably something like Alcoholics Anonymous with wheelchairs, which made me wonder how it was going to help me.

I wasn't particularly looking forward to going, but I sensed that it probably couldn't do me any harm to meet others on the ward, so I should give it a try. The minute I arrived at my first therapy session, however, I realized that I had just signed up for a club where I didn't want to be a member.

The ten other people in the room looked like survivors of an earthquake. Everyone was sitting in their wheelchairs, with braces around their necks. Two members of the group were hooked up to ventilators. Most of us were leaning off to one side. Either people looked afraid, or their eyes were glazed over with sadness. I wondered which expression was mine.

"OK, thank you all for coming," said the social worker, Bruce, opening his arms with a welcoming gesture. "As some of you already know, we like these sessions to be loose. You can talk about whatever you want to talk about. If you don't have something you'd like to discuss, I have some suggested topics."

It was clear that some people had been here longer than others and knew the routine.

The sole woman in the group spoke right away. "Well, I want to talk about how pointless all this talking is," she declared. "I don't want to talk about how I feel. I want to find out what I can do to get myself out of here."

Right away, I felt embarrassed for her. I didn't understand why she felt the need to be so aggressive. Her manner came across as unpleasant and prickly.

Bruce had obviously been well trained, because he maintained his tone of calm understanding.

"Does anyone else feel the same way as Mrs. Mulleavy?" he asked. "Let's talk about this."

But Mrs. Mulleavy wasn't done yet. "If I want to talk about anything, I want to talk about what experimental surgeries and studies are going on, and how I can sign up for them," she insisted.

"I agree," said one of the older members of the group, coming to Bruce's rescue. "I think we should talk about what we all know."

"Thank you, Mr. Klein," said Bruce. "Anyone want to share?"

Mr. Klein was the oldest in the group. His degree of injury was severe, but of all of us, he seemed to me to be the least shell-shocked. He had barely enough strength to push the joystick of the motorized chair, but his face was softened by graciousness. It turned out he had been injured in a car accident, on the way to visit his grandchildren.

"What about Belgium?" I asked. "The doctors told me that I wasn't well enough to go. But does anyone know if this is something you can do in two months' time, when you're feeling stronger?"

"Wait, what's Belgium?" asked another member of the group, who was breathing with the help of a ventilator.

Mr. Klein explained: "Apparently they use white blood cells and put them in the spinal cord to reduce swelling and improve recovery. It saves whatever axons you had that would normally be damaged without this kind of treatment."

"Why didn't anyone tell me about this?" said the man on the ventilator, whose name I later learned was Mr. Rodriguez.

No one wanted to say it, but it was obvious that Mr. Rodriguez hadn't been told about the surgery because of his level of injury, which was extremely severe. He had been injured in a cycling accident. What I grew to admire in Mr. Rodriguez was his determination to communicate, even if he could only get his words out when the machine was exhaling.

"Can someone tell me more?" he asked.

No one answered.

"I'm not an expert on this," said the social worker, stepping in to fill the silence. "Some of these questions you're going to have to ask your doctors."

"Does anyone know if the surgery still works when you've been injured for a longer period of time?" I wanted to know.

Again, no one knew the answer.

"I'm afraid I'm not very knowledgeable about this," Bruce repeated. "Maybe we can have a session where we talk about research next week when we've all had time to gather some more information?"

There were three other members of the group who had yet to speak up. Mr. Tam was an older Asian American man, in his seventies. I guessed he didn't talk so much because of the restrictions of his ventilator. By the look in his eyes, you could tell that he was listening and reacting to everything he heard, but when he tried to speak, it would take him so long to respond that he'd grow frustrated. At a certain point, you could see that it was easier for him to give up.

The two youngest members of the group barely spoke at all. Karl was twenty and injured from the shoulders down in a motorcycle accident. He was generally quiet and reserved, agreeing or disagreeing with someone else, but never initiating a change of subject. Eric, the youngest, had broken his neck riding an ATV. He had some mobility in his arms but nothing else. He rarely came to the sessions. I think it was all too much for him. At seventeen, he simply didn't have the emotional maturity to express how he thought or felt.

Of everyone in the group, Mrs. Mulleavy was the most vocal. She was in her late forties or early fifties. Injured in a car accident, she had a small amount of mobility in her arms. During our sessions, she contributed in short outbursts that often seemed unrelated to anything we'd been talking about before. When the social worker would ask her how she felt about something, she'd always snap back, "What do you mean, how do I feel? How do you think I feel?"

There was something about Mrs. Mulleavy that always made *me* feel wary, and I could see that other patients on the ward felt the same way, instinctively withdrawing from her. Nothing about her was welcoming. Her face naturally grimaced, even before she spoke. When she did smile, the smile would look forced. She seemed able to find the negative in everything. If you mentioned to her that it was nice to see the sun shining, she'd immediately say, "Haven't you heard the forecast? It's going to rain tomorrow." It was always raining in some part of the world for Mrs. Mulleavy. I came to the conclusion that while her injury had given her plenty to complain about, she probably complained a lot even *before* her injury.

Even though my instinct was to avoid Mrs. Mulleavy, I knew that on some level, I was feeling just as angry and confused. Everyone in the group came from different backgrounds, we were all at different points in our lives, and we had been injured in different ways, but even so, we had something in common: We had all been injured for as little as two months or less. None of us was able to process a change of this magnitude in such a short period of time. How do you start to take on board that you can no longer feel the majority of your body? How do you get used to the fact that you can no longer reach for a drink when you're thirsty? Or pick up the phone when you want to make a phone call, or even just go to the bathroom alone? How do you adjust to the idea that you're no longer going to be able to work or earn money? How do you begin to accept that any kind of physical relationship with someone is now out of the question? Or that you can no longer live alone? How do you make your brain understand all of this in the space of just a few short weeks? Our reactions were delayed and distorted by shock, and perhaps because of this, the therapy sessions could be extremely unpredictable. People were by turns philosophical, frantic, confused, strong, denying, affirming, angry, anxious, or just distracted. The newness of our injuries combined with the extent of our debilitation and our intense need to recover made for some tense moments. We all wanted to get better. At the same time, we all had those times in the day when we just wanted to give up altogether.

We had a bond, but it was a bond that none of us would have chosen. The two older gentlemen in the group, Mr. Klein in particular, were the most open and honest about what had happened. They didn't mask their emotions, and they tended to be particularly empathetic toward us younger members.

"For me to feel sad is nothing," I remember Mr. Klein saying to me once. "I have lived a long, great life. But to see someone as young as you, and to think of how much I have lived since I was your age, is what really upsets me."

Mr. Klein made a particular impression on me. I was sure that he had his moments of despair—just like we all did—but somehow he was able to reach out and connect with others. While Mrs. Mulleavy was constantly on the attack and Mr. Tam disappeared inside himself, Mr. Klein remained open. His room was always filled with guests, family members, and friends. He was a very good host, keeping up the conversation, putting others at ease. What I learned from Mr. Klein was that it was important to be gracious, especially in a situation where you were relying on others to such an enormous extent.

Despite my initial resistance to group therapy, I kept going. At least when I was there, I was around people who had been dealt the same hand. In our very different ways we were all trying to figure out how to play the next round.

7

Jumping the Curb

AFTER THE FIRST WEEK AT MOUNT SINAI, MY MOTORIZED wheelchair arrived. Although it was good to know I would be able to go places under my own steam, on another level, I didn't want to have anything to do with the chair. I didn't care about the chair. In fact, I just wanted to get up and walk away from the chair.

Larry, my physical therapist, showed me how to use it.

"Here's the On and Off button," he pointed out. "This is the joystick. You can use this to control the speed and change the direction. Here's Stop. Oh, and here's the horn." He pressed it jauntily. The horn made a pathetic *meep, meep* sound.

"It's OK," I said. "If I want people to get out of my way, I'll just scream."

Now that I had my own chair, I could participate in the wheelchair classes. The therapists set up cones along the hospital hallways and the patients had to steer around them.

The first time I drove the course, I maneuvered in and out of the cones without knocking any of them over.

"Oh my God, you're so good at driving your chair!" the therapists cheered.

I didn't know whether I should laugh or cry or both. All I had to do was press a button and steer. A three-year-old could do this. I had injured my body, not my mind. I wasn't an idiot. The humiliation of it all was stinging.

After the indoor obstacle course, we would have sessions outside. Here we had to learn how to "jump the curb." Larry would take us out on Fifth Avenue, and we would have to cross at the lights, then bump ourselves up onto the sidewalk on the other side. This sounds easy enough except that the curb at this particular point on the avenue was about five inches high.

"So here's what you do," Larry explained. "When you're about halfway across, you need to hit full speed. Then charge at the curb and keep going!"

Never mind that there were cars trying to turn onto the avenue. The first time I tried it, I'll admit, I was scared. The curb looked insurmountable. How does a wheelchair jump a five-inch curb? So I tried to follow Larry's instructions. I turned the speed up higher and kept going. As the front wheels hit the curb, the whole chair jolted, but I was up on the sidewalk.

"Cool!" said Larry. "Do it again, but faster."

We would wait for the red light and then go again. Passersby were staring at us. They had no idea what to make of this spectacle of a dozen people in wheelchairs and neck braces charging at the curb. Come to think of it, neither did we.

Then one morning, when I had been at Mount Sinai for a little more than a week, I woke up to find my grandmother sitting by my bedside, reading a magazine. I knew that her flight from Italy had arrived the night before, and I was expecting her, but I didn't know she would be there the moment I opened my eyes. I was so happy to see her, I felt tearful.

"Adesso stai bene. Sono qui." You're OK now. I'm here.

"Yes, you're here," I replied.

She must have been upset to see me like this, but even so, she kept the exact same look of love in her eyes that she had reserved for her grandchildren all our lives. She knew that I needed her to be strong, and so she exuded strength. There was no way I could explain to her how much better it made me feel that she had come. For the rest of my time at Mount Sinai, she would sit by my bed, reading her magazines, making sure that I had everything that I needed and that I never felt alone.

"Avrai fame?" she would ask. Are you hungry?

What concerned my grandmother most was that I had lost a lot of weight while in ICU. She was soon going to see about that. Every day, my grandmother and my mother would come to the hospital bringing freshly made lasagne, vegetables, and cake. Although I was missing our weekly family meals, just the fact that I was eating home-cooked food again gave me a feeling of being nourished and loved. As my grandmother unwrapped the aluminum foil from the top of each dish, my mouth watered at the smell of the Bolognese authenticity. My room became like a honey pot. Nurses arrived from every corner of the ward to try a bite of the Clark family dinner. My grandmother, who only speaks Italian, soon befriended all the nurses by offering them a taste. She would never allow a little thing like language to stand in the way of communicating, so she just went right ahead and spoke to them in Italian. Meanwhile, I wanted to rip the plates out of her hands and eat every morsel.

"Mamma mia! Checco!" my grandmother cried, using the diminutive of my name, as the piece of pasta she was feeding me slid out of the side of my mouth. I never minded when my grandmother fed me. It just seemed natural. She was wiping my mouth and giggling. "So you don't like it? We'll just put it all away."

"Then I'll bite you," I said. At least I still had control of my jaws.

Since I had moved to Mount Sinai, my room had become a whole lot busier. My brother had taken six weeks away from his office and was working by my hospital bed. My father came every night after he had finished work. Charlotte was on duty whenever my mom wasn't there. My mother spent every night with me, drowsing in a chair by my bed. My mom in particular was so strong, so capable, ready to take care of anything I needed. Yet there were signs of how much the shock was affecting her. Since my accident, she had lost her nerve. My mother, the strongest person I know, who always drove herself everywhere, just couldn't get behind the wheel anymore. My father and our family friends had to ferry her back and forth from the hospital.

One day I overheard a friend asking Charlotte how she was doing.

"What?" Charlotte replied, barely blinking. It was as if she had forgotten to think of herself, she was so focused on what was happening to me.

My brother, like the rest of the family, was on autopilot, grabbing whatever I needed the moment I asked for it, trying to find out about new research that was going on around the world, doing whatever he could. My dad said little, but his sad eyes spoke volumes. More than anyone else in the family, he knew exactly what was taking place in my body and how hard it was going to be for me to move forward.

Now that I was in Manhattan, my friends could come and visit, which was a definite improvement. Although I was always pleased to see people, I generally had to steel myself for the look on their faces when they first saw me. Their eyes went wide and they greeted me in a somewhat nervous, strained way.

"Heeeeey!"

Often, they didn't know what to say next. No one wanted to ask the simple question, "How are you?" because the answer was

obvious: I was sitting motionless in a wheelchair, wearing a neck brace. But it was hard to know what else to say. I think people were also thrown off by how diminished I looked. I used to be one of the tallest people in any room, but when I was sitting in the chair, suddenly I was so much shorter.

After we got over that initial blip, though, it was always great to see people and to catch up. I'd usually counteract any awkward pauses by asking people to tell me everything I'd missed in the past few weeks. Even if they felt badly recounting the mundane details of their lives, I kept encouraging them with my questions.

One of my most regular visitors to Mount Sinai was Suzan, a friend and colleague from when I worked at *Mademoiselle*.

The first time Suzan saw me, she did a better job than most of hiding her dismay.

"How are you?" she asked, without pause and with genuine concern.

I told her, "You know what? I'm great. I'm lucky to be here. Did you know I nearly died?"

"Francesco, tell me everything," she said.

We started to chat, easily, about what had happened to me. We realized that we'd both been so busy with our lives since I'd left *Mademoiselle* that we hadn't seen each other in almost a year. We had a lot to catch up on. Suzan had left the magazine and had just finished studying to be a yoga teacher. She promised to come back soon.

She did. On one of her subsequent visits, Charlotte was also with us.

"So, I wanted to ask you something," Suzan said.

"Fire away, Suz," I told her.

"Do you want to do yoga?"

I grinned from ear to ear. I had no idea what Suzan had in mind, I just knew I was game.

"Charlotte, shut the door!" I instructed my sister.

"So, as part of my yoga training, I've been learning about breathing techniques," Suzan told me. "I've also been working on how to translate that into helping you with your breathing. But I wanted to check it was OK with you before going any further." As she said this, she moved her chair closer to my bed. She'd pulled out a notebook, filled with her handwriting. She had been preparing for this for a while.

"Of course I'll try whatever you want to show me," I responded. At this point I could use whatever help I could get. After my accident, I'd lost all neurological function to control the muscles below my shoulders, and this included the muscles necessary for breathing. I only had about 60 percent of my lung capacity. My left lung had collapsed from taking in water in the swimming pool, and from being unable to cough up the liquid. Although my singing had helped to strengthen my diaphragm, my breathing was still dangerously shallow.

"I don't want to overwhelm you right away," Suzan explained. "So let's take this very slowly."

We decided to focus on positive thinking and relaxation to begin with. This was fine by me. I wanted to do anything that would help diffuse the underlying panic that was with me at all times of the day and night. Suzan got me to close my eyes and imagine I was going for a walk outside. As I breathed in, I pictured the color green, and this made me feel more peaceful; as I breathed out, I imagined the color red, which was going to help me to expel negativity and stress. After I had been doing this exercise for a few minutes, I found that when I opened my eyes again, I had the feeling of being refreshed, as if I had temporarily left the confines of my bed, my room, and my body.

Then we began to work specifically on my breathing. Suzan was going to teach me how to breathe more fully again. We worked on strengthening my diaphragm. She wanted me to focus on imagining my breath entering and filling my left lung, the one that had collapsed. She was going to try to reconnect me with my intercostals, the muscles between each rib that help you to inhale and exhale fully. I had to try to inhale from the bottom of my diaphragm, then through my midsection and then all the way to my eyeballs. This was practically impossible for me. I could only try to do this for about thirty seconds before I had to rest. But over time, my strength began to improve, and I could see that the exercises were helping. After doing my breathing exercises, I felt as if I had more energy. I enjoyed feeling productive. Even while lying flat on my back, I had found a way to help build up my muscles while getting an optimal amount of oxygen to my cells, so that hopefully I would never have to be on a ventilator again. Like the singing, the breathing exercises were a way of taking my recovery into my own hands, doing whatever I could to get better.

Suzan had also alerted me to one of the biggest lessons of my injury: I could no longer function alone. I was completely dependent on others to help me, even with my breathing. This meant I had to begin to learn to accept help, and to accept it graciously. It began at Mount Sinai. Suzan teaching me "yoga." My grandmother sitting at my bedside, calming me with her presence, bringing me food. My mother and father and their constant focus on my needs and recovery. My siblings and their ability to keep treating me as their brother, no matter how much had changed. All the nurses and aides who facilitated my days. It was a daunting and humbling experience, but perhaps it helped that I couldn't believe that the situation was permanent. Yes, I needed help now, but surely I'd become my independent self again soon. Maybe in a few months, or a year, everything would return to normal. It had to. I couldn't imagine it any other way.

8

꧁

Madonna

I HAD BEEN AT MOUNT SINAI FOR OVER A MONTH, BUT IT was beginning to feel like years. Every day merged slowly into the next, each one following an identical sequence. Because my days were so predictable, one day stands out above all the others. It was a Tuesday in July, and I was in the middle of stretching my arms and legs in the physical-therapy room. Larry was holding out my left leg as I lay on the mat with my arms strapped to inflatable splints. The splints kept my arms from being constantly curled up by straightening them out temporarily. They also made me look like the Michelin Man.

Looking up from the mat, I noticed a group of people walking down the hallway toward the physical-therapy room. I thought they were probably some friends visiting Mr. Klein, who always had the most visitors. I tried to refocus on my arm stretches, but then I realized that the crowd outside the therapy room was actually my brother and sister, my mother, Suzan, and about a half dozen of my former colleagues from the *Harper's Bazaar* team.

"How are all of you here? Why aren't you at work? It's two o'clock!"

"We . . . it's slow today," my friend Anna, a fellow assistant from *Bazaar*, informed me. "Anyway, you need to go to your room right now." The whole group was acting strangely, even my mom and siblings. Everyone seemed kind of rushed and anxious. Something was up, but I had no idea what.

"Why?" I asked, puzzled. "Am I in trouble?"

"No. There's this doctor who will be calling you . . . from Israel," Charlotte blurted. "He wants to speak with you about something, and he's calling in fifteen minutes."

Larry and Cynthia were obviously in on whatever it was, because they were nodding in agreement with my sister.

"What are you up to?" I protested. "There's no way a doctor from Israel is calling me now. It's midnight there." I scanned their faces, searching for a smile or a face about to crack. Nobody was budging.

"Even so," said Anna. "You need to be in your room *now*. C'mon."

Larry and Cynthia were already transferring me back into my chair, which was weird, because they didn't even ask any questions about why I was ending therapy early.

"OK. We just need to transf—uff."

Larry picked me up and plopped me into the chair. Transfer done in ten seconds flat. It normally took ten minutes, and that was on a good day. My back hit the seatback of the wheelchair with a soft thud. Now I was completely out of sorts.

"What the—?"

But there was no time to even finish asking the question, because Cynthia was already pushing me out of the therapy room at such a pace that my hair was practically blowing in the wind. The other patients looked up enviously at me as I left. You never left therapy early unless you had a very good excuse to do so.

As I departed, Mr. Klein quipped, "Can I go too?"

As soon as I got to my room, Larry and Cynthia transferred me into my bed.

"Guys . . . can I just have a minute to catch my—"

Too late. Larry and Cynthia picked me up *again,* and gently tossed me into the bed.

"Breath?"

And then the phone rang. Anna answered and handed the phone to Charlotte, who held it up to my ear.

"Is this Francesco?"

"Yes . . . hi?" I was confused; I had no idea who it was on the other end of the line. It certainly didn't sound like an Israeli doctor.

"This is Madonna," said the voice on the phone.

"Ha! No, no it isn't!" Doctor, my ass, I was thinking, looking over at my friends and my sister.

"Yessss, yes it is," she replied sternly. Suddenly, I got it. This was definitely her. Her voice was unmistakable; I'd heard it so many times before. Madonna, the icon, was actually on the other end of the phone. It was surreal, as if I was listening to her on the radio, except that when I spoke, she answered.

My sister, who was holding the phone, mouthed, "Madonna called you!"

"*Heeeeey!* I'm such a big fan," I told her. "I saw you in concert twice last year. Fantastic."

"Thank you so much," Madonna replied. "I was sorry to hear about your accident." Suddenly, the icon was human.

"Yeah. I hit my chin . . ."

"The most important thing for you to do now is surround yourself with your family and people that love you." If she could see me now, I thought. I looked around the room at the faces of all my family members, friends, and therapists, standing there gaping at me, their jaws on the ground. My tiny room was packed.

I answered, "Yes, I am. I am so lucky to not be alone."

"That support is what you need."

I told her how much I appreciated her calling. Then I thought to myself, Well, how often do you get to talk to Madonna? so I figured I'd try to keep her on the line. I'd read somewhere that she'd just appeared in a play in London, so I thought I'd ask her something about that.

"So, do you prefer concerts, film, television, or theater? I heard you just did this play . . ."

"Theater is so different because you have one shot to get it right in front of the audience," Madonna replied. Wow, I was having a conversation with *Madonna*. Even so, I wasn't nervous. Truth be told, I had almost died one month earlier, so in the bigger scheme of things, you could have put me on the phone with the pope, and I probably would have answered, "Yo, Papa-P. How's Rome?"

"I assisted Arianne Phillips on the last shoot she styled for *Bazaar*," I said, mentioning Madonna's personal stylist. "She is such a talent, and an incredible person. You must love working with her." As it turned out, it was Arianne who had contacted Madonna about my injury and had helped to coordinate this call.

We chatted for a while longer. Before we finished speaking, Madonna told me something that has stayed in my mind ever since: "Focus on the positive and surround yourself with supportive people," she said. The conversation ended, and my sister hung up the phone.

"I can't believe it," Charlotte said. "You two spoke as if you knew each other from elementary school!"

"Soooooo, what's for dinner?" I replied with a grin.

"Oh, no. You talk. You talk right now!" Charlotte insisted.

"Well, she was really nice," I replied.

Everyone in my room was still staring at me. They all had a

slightly glazed expression on their faces, and they were leaning in toward me, their mouths agape.

"I never noticed how sharp all of your teeth were until right now. And so white and shiny," I teased.

"That's it? She's nice? Are you kidding me?" Suzan said as she mimed choking me to death. "You will speak!"

Suzan is never starstruck by anyone—she's met and interviewed countless celebrities for her work in magazines. But even calm and collected Suzan turned to jelly at the mere mention of the Material Girl.

It was fun to tease Suzan and my sister, but the truth was, I was blown away that Madonna had called, and that my friends had made this happen. Before everyone left, I thanked them for arranging such a great surprise. In the coming days, when I felt at all low, I would think to myself, Well, it's not everyone who gets to chat with Madonna. Back then, I assumed that this was probably the first and last time our paths would cross. Little did I know.

9

Mrs. Mulleavy

THE MORE TIME I SPENT IN THE REHAB WARD, THE MORE I was faced with the double-bind familiar to every new spinal-cord-injury patient. Your natural assumption is that you're going to get better. You're constantly being told that you can't.

My main doctor was a man I'll call Dr. Ford. At the beginning of my time at the hospital, I was impressed by his good bedside manner. He had an air of calm authority and when he walked into the room, I had the sense that he was firmly in control of his universe. Unlike my doctor at the ICU, who had been so cold and steely, Dr. Ford was talkative and charming and seemed like he wanted to help.

"I was sorry to hear that you weren't eligible for the Belgium research," he told me when I'd first found out I wouldn't be allowed to receive this experimental surgery.

"That's fine," I said. "I understand that it wasn't possible this time."

"Still, I wouldn't feel too bad about it," he went on. "From what I've seen, they're not showing any measurable results."

At this point, I assumed Dr. Ford was trying to downplay things so I wouldn't feel too disappointed.

The next time I saw him, I made sure to ask him about any other research that was going on in the world.

"Well, there are some trials going on," said Dr. Ford, "but I have to tell you that at this point, none of it has been very promising. And we don't want you to get your hopes up."

"It's not that I'm getting my hopes up," I replied. "I just want to know about all the options that are available to me."

Then next time I saw Dr. Ford, I asked him again if there was anything else I could be doing.

"Francesco," he said, using the tone an adult uses to placate a child, "we see patients here all the time, and they all want to know what's going on with new research and surgeries. We feel that it's very important not to give people false hope. The most important thing to think about right now is how you're going to move on with your life. You need to focus on adapting to your injury. That's the most important thing right now."

OK, I got it. His only advice was to "move on." But I didn't know what it meant to move on with my life. Move on? Where? What was I going to do? Get a new job? I couldn't even brush my own teeth.

One day, Dr. Ford came to my room to tell me about a new surgery he wanted me to consider. My eyes lit up. He'd brought a video with him so that I could learn about the specifics of the procedure. The video outlined the benefits of something called tendon transfer, which involves cutting a tendon from a working muscle and redirecting it to a paralyzed muscle.

"After you have this surgery," Dr. Ford told me, "you'll be able to flip your wrist up, then clench your fingers into a claw so you can pick something up."

He said this as if he were recounting a miracle.

"Is this kind of surgery reversible?" I wanted to know.

"No, it's not reversible. But it does mean that you'll be able to pick things up by yourself, which is a very good goal to have."

"Well, what happens if I get some mobility back in my fingers naturally?"

"If you did get mobility back, and you'd already had the tendon transfer, you most likely wouldn't be able to move that area because those tendons would have been severed."

"Then I don't think I want to do that," I told him. I wanted to heal and get better. I didn't want to do something that was going to cut a tendon that might actually work.

I had already learned that after the swelling in the spine decreases, many people with spinal-cord injuries see a degree of improvement in their mobility in the course of the first year or so. I knew that my chances were pretty slender. There was still a degree of the unknown as to what would happen after the swelling subsided, and no one could dispute that. In a week, a month, or a year—no one knew—I might get back some more function. I felt it was my job to keep my body in the best condition possible so that I would have a chance to benefit from that mobility if and when it returned.

But Dr. Ford remained determined to play down anything that sounded at all hopeful. What he didn't realize was that I needed to hear something—anything—from him that was positive, to help get me through this. Instead, he continued to lay out the worst-case scenario: "Don't expect to get better." Would it really be so terrible to make me feel like it was possible to improve? What if Dr. Ford was wrong, like the ICU doctor had been wrong when he told me that I'd never be able to breathe without a ventilator? And ultimately, if there was so much that was unknown about spinal-cord injuries, then how could anyone ever be so certain?

It's not that I don't have respect for doctors. I do. I come from a long line of physicians. My dad is a doctor. I grew up in a household where a typical conversation started around the family dinner table was: "So there's this new heart medication coming on the market, but it seems it could be really bad for your liver." And so *because* I come from a family of physicians, I know that doctors can be fallible. I know that science itself is in a perpetual state of evolution and even the best doctor in the world can only know so much. Yes, I was terrified at the prognosis I had been given, but there was still a part of me that wanted to say to Dr. Ford, "Well, I'm sure you're giving me your educated opinion, but ultimately, you really can't know what the future will bring." Even if he wasn't prepared to say anything that was positive, at least he could say, "I don't really know."

What's more, I was discovering that the attitude of my therapists was exactly the same as Dr. Ford's.

One day, Cynthia came into my room with a new idea to try. She was carrying some pieces of cloth and small splints. "When you sleep at night, I want you to wear this special splint that will tie your fingers closed shut," she explained. "What's going to happen is it will make your tendons tighten up. What's great is that your fingers will contract into a fist position, which means you'll be able to grasp things."

"Does this mean I can never straighten them again?" I wanted to know.

"That's right!" she told me happily. "But the most important thing is that you can grab things, right?"

My immediate reaction was to refuse. I didn't want to have my hands permanently clenched. But by now I was beginning to question myself. Maybe I was wrong about this. Maybe these people were right. They were the experts, after all. Maybe I should just do what Cynthia was suggesting. It wasn't like it was surgery. Maybe this would help.

Although I was reluctant, I let Cynthia persuade me to try the splints. She wrapped up my hands and left me with two bound fists resting on the bed cover.

Later that evening, my mother arrived for her evening shift.

"What happened to your hands?" she asked right away.

"Cynthia says this will help them form a fist, so I can pick things up."

My mother reacted without hesitation. She quickly began unwrapping the binding, carefully pulling my fingers free and massaging them straight again.

"You're going to heal, Francesco," she told me emphatically. "I don't want to see your hands like that ever again."

The longer I stayed at the hospital, the more frustrated I became with my doctors and therapists, the very people who were supposed to be helping me. I was going to therapy each day, but I no longer felt as if I was getting anything useful from the exercises. In every session, we worked on mat transfers. We worked on strengthening and straightening my arms where I already had some mobility. But we never worked on my legs besides stretching them every now and again. Meanwhile, my body was changing before my very eyes. I had lost a lot of muscle in my arms already and in my fingers. My forearms were as thin and flat as two wooden planks, the bones covered in limp, flabby skin. My fingers were skinny and lifeless; they had already lost the firmness that comes from use. I had gone from having the body of a fit and healthy twenty-four-year-old, to feeling like I was wasting away and shriveling into a corpse. I was afraid to look at myself. I avoided my reflection in the bathroom, and averted my eyes from the big mirror in the therapy room. But even without seeing my reflection, I knew what was going on. The same thing that was happening to me was happening to all the other patients on the ward. We were wasting away.

My instinct was to keep working my body so that I could retain as much muscle tone as possible in case I got function back at a later point. I wanted to keep my joints from freezing up from lack of use. I felt that it was extremely important to work on my legs in particular, as I had no sensation there whatsoever. But when I raised this concern with Cynthia, she told me that this wasn't a priority.

"You need to get to a point where you can leave this hospital and move on with your life, Francesco."

There it was, that phrase again. Moving on with my life. I hated it.

I'm sure the doctors and nurses probably thought that patients like me were angry because of our injuries, so we were taking our anger out on others, but it was a whole lot more complicated than that. Everywhere we looked, we were faced with professionals who didn't believe we could get better. No one seemed focused on helping us to heal. Everything that happened in the ward was predicated on the assumption that the situation was hopeless. The attitude of the therapists was, Well, here goes nothing! We can't really help you, but we have to try something, so we'll do this with you for a while, but then you're going to have to move along so we can deal with the next hopeless case. Meanwhile, my mind was racing in the opposite direction. I was asking myself the kinds of questions that anyone in my situation would ask. How do I get myself out of this? How do I fix this? What do I do next to help myself?

Even so, there were many days when I just didn't have the stamina to stand my ground against the negativity. I got exhausted. I felt beaten down and dispirited. Every time I brought up my hope of getting mobility back, my doctors and therapists would look at me with a mix of condescension and pity.

"Give up. You're just making things harder for yourself," the look seemed to say.

One evening, my dad came by after work.

"You know, the doctors and therapists here don't think I can get better," I told him. Until now, we'd avoided having this conversation. Even to say it out loud would feel like admitting defeat.

"I know," my dad said without skipping a beat. "But they don't know you."

"It's just that sometimes I think it would be easier to agree with them," I pointed out.

"Francesco, I know how hard this is," he told me. "But you mustn't get discouraged. My whole career, I've been told that vitamins and homeopathy don't do anything, and now all the research is showing that the opposite is true. I've seen people who've been told they have six months to live, who live for six years. We're going to figure this out. We're going to do this together."

It seemed to me I had two options. I could listen to the doctors who had told me my situation was hopeless and do nothing. Or I could try to do whatever I could to move forward with the help of my family. My injury was not a disease. It didn't have to be degenerative. If I worked hard, I didn't see why I shouldn't be able to make progress. Christopher Reeve had been in the news ever since he had been paralyzed in a riding accident seven years prior, and I knew that he believed that he could get better and heal. It was extremely inspiring to me to know that he was optimistic about his future, and that he had begun to regain some movement. As a celebrity, he was bringing so much attention to people with SCI, promoting new medical research into these kinds of injuries any way he could. Surely it was inevitable that at some point, someone would come up with a cure.

Christopher Reeve was a beacon of hope for all of us in the rehab ward. While I was still at Mount Sinai, the word went around that there was going to be a special about him on television. That afternoon, you could hear everyone's TV sets running in sync.

The documentary chronicled Mr. Reeve's progress over the past two years. The filmmakers showed him suspended in a harness, his legs dangling over a treadmill. Therapists were at his sides, and they were guiding his legs in a walking motion. He was moving. Yes, he was being helped, but he was walking! It turned out he was participating in a research study designed to assess the effect of exercise on paralyzed patients, using treadmills to see if this kind of exercise could aid recovery of function.

Most impressively, it looked like the exercise theory was helping. Although Mr. Reeve had been told that his injury was complete and that he would never move or feel again, he now had motion in his right wrist; he was getting sensation back in his left fingers and both legs. It was such a contrast from the therapy room at Mount Sinai, where everyone was basically lying still throughout the session. I knew right away I wanted to be much more aggressive about the kind of therapy I was doing. I wanted to get up and running again.

The next day at therapy, I was excited to talk to Cynthia about the TV program. It turned out she hadn't even watched it.

"It was amazing," I told her. "He was walking on a treadmill with a harness, and therapists were helping him. I mean, he was really walking."

"Well, it's interesting," Cynthia replied right away, "but you know it's not clear that there are real benefits."

OK, how did Cynthia know there weren't any real benefits to new research unless she was prepared to give it a chance? How can science ever move forward if no one's ever open to trying something new? She hadn't even watched the program.

"What I want to know is when can I start working on my legs and my lower body like that?" I asked.

"That's experimental," said Cynthia. "It's body-weight-supported gait training."

"There doesn't seem to be anything experimental about it at all, really," I pointed out. "It seems very logical that you would have to do some sort of walking in order to retrain your legs."

"It looks interesting. There need to be a lot of therapists to assist, and there's a lot of prep time."

"So? I want to do that."

To Cynthia, if I couldn't feel a part of my body, it didn't exist. My back, my stomach, my legs were irrelevant. We never did anything to work on those areas. I couldn't understand this reasoning. It seemed logical to me that if a part of my body wasn't responding, we should focus *more* time on it, not less. If nothing else, it would foster muscle tone so that I didn't shrivel up completely.

"Francesco, you have to understand," said Cynthia, her tone finally losing its incessant strain of merriment, "I don't want to give you false hope."

I had heard this argument one too many times. These people truly believed it would be better for me to expect nothing rather than be disappointed. They never took the time to think about things from my point of view. I was twenty-four years old, and my life had just been shattered into thousands of pieces. What would be so wrong about having hope? Hope was the one thing that was keeping me going.

All of a sudden, I had a feeling of intense claustrophobia. I just wanted to get out of that place; I wanted to go somewhere where people understood me. I didn't want to lie there on a mat getting my arms stretched. Cynthia never seemed to understand my urgency to take the next step. She set the goals for me, and then she would look disdainfully at me whenever I asked to go beyond her prescribed limits. She might have seen a lot of patients with SCI, but she had never been in the position of the person on the mat, trying to figure out how to survive this. I wanted to do whatever I could to help scientists to fix these kinds of injuries. Above all, I wanted to get up and walk. *That's* what I wanted to work on.

I wasn't the only one who was reaching a breaking point. That week, halfway through group therapy, Mrs. Mulleavy erupted into a kind of spontaneous fury.

"I *hate* it here!" she spat, looking daggers at the therapist. "All of the therapists are incompetent; they're the most unintelligent people I have ever met. I don't even know why we have to come to these therapy sessions. What's there to talk about?"

She was bright red, and spittle was flying out of her mouth. This wasn't a person who was just a little angry. I felt as if I was watching someone on television screaming in one of those court dramas. My first instinct was to appease her in some sort of way, to distract her, to calm her down. Bruce, the social worker, beat me to it.

"Well, that's one of the reasons for these therapy sessions," he intoned. "We have no criteria on what we should talk about, so if you want to express concerns about your therapy routines, then—"

"It has nothing to do with that," interrupted Mrs. Mulleavy, who was unstoppable at this point. "I think you're all idiots, and I'm wasting my time in this hospital doing nothing."

"So what do you want to do?" I asked. I wasn't challenging her opinion. I actually wanted to know what else she thought we could be doing that would make our time here more productive.

"I don't want to spend hour upon hour getting from my chair to the mat and from the mat to the chair. I want to learn how to walk again!"

This I understood. I found myself nodding in agreement. I could see that others in the group were beginning to do the same.

Mrs. Mulleavy was saying things that we all thought and felt but for whatever reason, we didn't feel able to voice. Sure, the therapists and doctors were well-meaning and treated us kindly enough, but the fact remained that they had given up on us. I had gone from being horrified by Mrs. Mulleavy to being in complete agreement with her.

A few days after Mrs. Mulleavy's outburst, I was in the occupational-therapy room, working on picking up various small objects with my fingers. Since I couldn't really move my fingers, this was almost impossible for me. It was as if I was trying to use a giant spatula to pick up a dime. Every attempt was clumsy and ineffective, and I was growing frustrated. One of the aides noticed that I was struggling and came over to me.

"Did you hear what happened to Mrs. Mulleavy?" the aide asked.

"Did she buy a stun gun to use on the doctors?" I speculated. "She did, didn't she? She shot the social worker!"

"She left," the aide informed me. "Everything's cleared out of her room; she went last night."

It turned out that Mrs. Mulleavy had checked out to go to the Kessler Institute for Rehabilitation in New Jersey. We had all heard of it because Christopher Reeve had gone there, and it was known to be one of the best. Suddenly, I wanted to pack my bags and follow her. What were they doing over there in New Jersey that was so great? What kinds of therapy was I missing by staying here at Mount Sinai? What if Mrs. Mulleavy progressed faster than me, got more finger mobility, or began to regain more sensation in her body? How would that make me feel? And then it hit me. What if Mrs. Mulleavy got better while I was put out to pasture?

The people who worked at the hospital were constantly cautioning us to think small, to limit our expectations, so that we could learn to live with our existing situation. Even a simple and straightforward question such as "How can I get better?" was too provocative for our doctors and therapists. But Mrs. Mulleavy found this unacceptable. When someone asked her in therapy, "What do you want to work on?" she would say, "I want to work on walking." When the social worker asked her, "What do you want to talk about today?" she would say, "I want to talk about how I can get up out of this chair and walk out of this room."

It was easy to criticize her approach, but you couldn't fault her passion. Mrs. Mulleavy's rage kept pushing her forward. She was constantly asking herself what needed to happen in order to fix the problem. I didn't like the way she went about it, but at least she wasn't falling into the trap of complacency, passivity, or despair. She might have been a pain in the ass, but at least she had a plan.

〜〜✻〜〜

10

Moving On

I REMAINED AT MOUNT SINAI FOR OVER TWO MONTHS. BE-
fore I left the hospital, despite everyone's naysaying, I actually
got some more movement back.

I was getting showered at the time. The aide was performing
the usual routine, washing me down. While he was soaping me, I
had the shampoo bottle on my lap, and all of a sudden it slipped
and fell to the floor. Without thinking about it, I instinctively
went to grab the bottle. Rationally I knew that I couldn't reach
for the bottle anymore, but my brain was so accustomed to firing
off commands that it just went ahead and did so. Suddenly, my
right wrist twitched.

"Wait? Did I just see that?" I thought.

And then it twitched again. And again, and again. I thought I
was hallucinating.

"Holy cow! Look!" I said to the aide.

I moved my wrist some more. I couldn't stop. I didn't want to
stop, for fear of not knowing what it felt like to make my wrist
move ever again.

"All right!" he told me. "See, you're getting better! Keep doing it!"

We were both laughing.

"Now I'll try the left one," I said, and it moved too! Yes! Ha!

I knew that my parents would be coming to see me before the end of the day, and I couldn't wait to show them my progress. After the shower, the aide got me dressed and put me back to bed. I lay there, willing my parents to hurry up and walk through the door. Anyone who happened to pass my room that evening heard me calling out, "Hey, look! I can move my wrists! Check it out!"

When my parents finally arrived that evening, I actually waved hello to them. My mom and dad were so happy, you would think I'd just won the Nobel Peace Prize. We were all elated. This tiny improvement meant a great deal to us. If I could use my wrists, then who knows what else I would be able to get back? I had already done something I'd been told I wouldn't be able to do, and this was incredibly gratifying.

The next morning, I couldn't wait to get to therapy and tell Cynthia the good news. And while she was initially excited for me, there was something about her tone that seemed determined to "bring me back down to earth."

"Great!" she said. "The swelling in your spine must be going down, and the nerves are now able to work."

"So, then if more of the swelling subsides, I'll probably get back more function, right?"

"Maybe," she replied hesitantly. "It's exciting, right?" but the tone in her voice said otherwise. I was pretty certain that if she was the one sitting in the wheelchair, and she got some movement back in her wrists, then she would be downright ecstatic. But for whatever reason, she preferred to play it cool. OK, Cynthia, I thought. I don't need your approval. I've already proven to myself that I can get better.

Yes, I was having to deal with the prevailing negativity hovering over the rehab ward, but I was also having to contend with another specter: money. My insurance company was paying for my treatment and therapy for the moment, but not indefinitely. At some point, the line would be drawn. But when? For my first month in the hospital, I was in the dark about it. I heard from my patient advocate, Jack, that he was negotiating with my insurance representative, but until the matter was cleared up, no one could say for sure when I would have to leave.

Then, toward the end of my first month, I found out I could stay one more month, until the beginning of August. Suddenly I had a window of just a few weeks to plan for the next step. We were scrambling to figure it all out. I knew that in order to continue with my therapy, I needed to become an outpatient at a hospital near to my parents' house, where I would be living. At this point, I was still under the assumption that someone at Mount Sinai would *tell* me what to do—"Here's what everyone does after they leave here"—and then I would go ahead and do it. But when that didn't happen, I started to worry.

"What about Burke in Westchester?" I asked my therapists, mentioning a local hospital with a rehabilitation department. "At least it isn't too far from my home."

"Yeah, Burke isn't bad," they would say without much enthusiasm. "You could do your outpatient therapy there."

"Well, then maybe I should focus on the Kessler Institute, even though that's in New Jersey?"

"They're both good. I'm sure you'd be fine at both places. It's really up to you."

Not bad? Both good? I needed more than this. I wanted an actual opinion so I could make an informed decision. But when I asked others at the hospital, I got similar responses: "You can do that if you want," was the general tone. It felt like the underlying message was, "Well, you're not going to get better, so it doesn't really matter where you go." I was beginning to realize that there was no preordained next step and that after I left Mount Sinai, I was going to be on my own.

I was very fortunate to have my family to help with the research, to inform, support, and guide me. Without them, I would have been lost. I was also lucky that my patient advocate, Jack, was one of the few people I met at the hospital who understood how I felt. Jack was also in a wheelchair due to a spinal-cord injury. It was easy to talk to him about the challenges I was facing, because he had faced them himself. He'd also dealt with hundreds of patients in the same circumstances.

"Where do I go from here?" I wanted to know. "I've been here a month, and I've got one more month to go. I'm nowhere near ready to take this next step."

Jack gave me a look that told me he knew exactly how hard it could be. Then he told me something that nearly blew me out of my chair. "You know, five years ago you would have stayed in an inpatient recovery hospital like this one for five or six months."

"Huh?"

"It's only because health insurance doesn't cover as much as it used to that you can only stay for two months. That is what is limiting everyone's time here."

"You're kidding me. . . ."

"Basically, your insurance covers the same amount of therapy as someone who has broken a foot or a knee."

I couldn't believe what I was hearing. Two months wasn't nearly enough time for those patients who had breathing problems and were bedridden the first couple of weeks to adequately recover. It didn't seem fair to any of us, but that's the way it was, and no one, with the exception of Mrs. Mulleavy, seemed to have the guts to point out the insanity of the system.

As my departure date loomed, I began to worry more and more. I couldn't even begin to imagine how my parents and siblings were going to be able to look after me on their own. At the hospital I had three nurses, two doctors, two aides, and three therapists, all attending to my needs. There were people to transfer me from the bed to the chair, to take me to therapy, to shower me, to change my catheter, to help me in the bathroom, to feed me, and to do all the hundred and one things I needed each day. Now my family was going to have to take care of me without any of this support. How were they going to manage it?

"So, who in your family wants to learn how to cath you?" one of the nurses asked one day.

My mother, my sister, and my brother were all in the room. We were taken aback by the question. I think it brought home for all of us that we needed to start getting ready for the transition from hospital care to family care.

"Not me!" my brother Mike said immediately. It was as if he'd realized he was the obvious candidate for the job but that he did not want to be considered.

"I'll learn," said my sister right away. It's no coincidence that my sister is the only one of the siblings to go into the medical profession.

Together with my mother, my sister watched carefully as the nurse demonstrated how to attach the long, clear bag and the tube. Yes, I was embarrassed about being exposed in front of my family. I hadn't been naked in front of them since I was a kid. But on the other hand, there was no one else in the world I could ask to do this for me.

"OK, that's easy," said my sister confidently. "It's no big deal."

The nurse covered me up.

After the nurse left, my brother apologized. "I'm sorry that I can't do that for you," he said. "I just can't."

"I understand," I told him. "It is what it is." For a while, my brother had thought he wanted to be a doctor, but he knew he would have lasted exactly five minutes. He was just too squeamish.

Even so, the incident with the catheter only served to remind me how much this was going to affect all of us. Yes, I was the one who had been injured, but every member of my family was going to have to modify their lives in order to give me the help I needed.

My last full day at the hospital, I was in tears. My brother was there with me.

"I don't want to go home," I told him. "I don't want to do this to Mom and Dad. I don't want to be a burden to them."

"Don't feel bad, you could never be a burden," Mike told me.

"But that's how it feels," I said.

"Why? What makes you feel that way?"

"I just don't know how we're going to do this," I said. "How am I even going to take a shower?"

"We built the new shower downstairs for you, remember?" my brother reminded me.

"How is Mom going to do her work and take care of me?"

"It's not just going to be Mom. It's going to be all of us. I'm going to come over every day after work."

"How am I going to get to therapy? What therapy am I even going to do?"

"There's so much that we are going to do. There's Burke, there's Kessler. We're going to do everything we can." My brother reached for all the pages he had printed out, articles about rehabilitation hospitals and research trials. He couldn't handle the catheter, but he could do this work for me and he could be there for me when I needed him most.

Even so, I was leaving, and I was scared. My whole life I had always known what came next. Now it felt as if I was heading straight for a big black hole.

11

Adaptation

I HAD BEEN IN THE HOSPITAL FOR NEARLY THREE MONTHS, living in a room without a view from the window or anything else to relieve the monotony. My family home is an old house with lots of character, gables, a porch, a little verandah on the back, set amidst shrubs and trees. Driving back from the hospital that day, I could picture my mom's kitchen, the hub of the house, a big pan of Bolognese ragu stewing on the stove and water already bubbling for pasta. There is no place in the world I know better, or where I feel more comfortable.

And then we turned into the drive.

There was no missing it. Right at the front of the house, extending the entire length of the left side of the building was a large wooden wheelchair ramp about fifty feet long leading up to the front porch.

"Oh, no," I blurted. "Look what you did!"

My eyes started to fill with tears.

It was as if someone had hung a massive banner across the entire house emblazoned with the words FRANCESCO SCREWED UP.

I knew my mother and father worked hard to make sure the house was ready for me, but I couldn't feel pleased. I felt crushed.

"You ruined it," was all I could think to myself. "You ruined your family's house. You ruined their lives, and your life. You are an idiot."

"*This* is temporary, Checco," said my mother, seeing the look on my face. "You won't need this ramp or this chair for very long."

Suddenly, I wasn't just crying, I was sobbing loudly. I had never felt so loved and cared for as I did at that very moment, but because of that, I also felt guilty. How was I going to repay my family for everything they were sacrificing for me? Life had seemed so easy before my injury: do well in school, be strong and independent, and be there for your family. I'd graduated from college, got my foot on the career ladder; I'd just been offered and had accepted this new job that was a great promotion. Now what did I have to show for it all? A chair. A ramp. And a world of pain and anxiety to my family.

I remembered all the times I had come home in the past, running up to the front door, pushing it open and racing right in. Now my dad was pushing *me* up a ramp in a chair. My sister must have heard us come home, because she was already waiting at the door to welcome us. She bent down to hug me, but this time I couldn't hug back.

Inside, I immediately looked to the stairway, which led to the second floor and to my bedroom. Would I ever be able to get up those stairs?

"Don't worry, Checco," said my mom, reading my mind, "we have everything set up for you."

She pushed me into the living room. I was expecting the usual, elegant arrangement of sofas, side tables, and lamps. Instead there was a giant ugly metal hospital bed right in the middle of the room. Next to it was a lift—a sort of miniature crane—so that I would be able to get from my wheelchair into the bed. All the regular furniture was pushed up against the walls.

My mother could see that I was upset. She tried to make me smile. "Oh, we never used this room so much anyway," she joked. But I felt mortified.

"Thanks, Mom," I tried. "I'm sure I'll get used to it."

I wasn't the only one who was going to have to get used to the new setup. My entire family was having to adjust. In the following days, we had to figure out so many things: how to dress and undress me, get me showered, get me to the bathroom, keep me cathed, move me from the chair to the bed . . . Everyone worked hard to appear upbeat and to figure things out.

Everything was a production, but the biggest production of all was getting me in and out of the car. My parents were borrowing a special van from one of my dad's patients who had multiple sclerosis, so that they could drive me around. It was a huge, white Chevy that looked a lot like the van on *The A-Team,* except for the giant lift on the back to accommodate my chair. First, I had to be wheeled onto the lift. Then my chair had to be tied down with multiple straps. After the four straps had been tied to the four corners of my chair, there was somehow always one strap left over. Even with all our combined college degrees, we couldn't figure it out.

"Maybe the extra strap is for your big nose?" my brother suggested helpfully.

Then the lift would wheeze me up into the back of the van, but once inside, I just didn't have the trunk stability to sit up properly. The van swayed like a boat with the slightest curve on the road and meanwhile I'd get thrown about like a kid on an amusement park ride. After a while, whoever was driving learned to warn me when we were going to turn so I could prepare myself. Even me sitting in the back of a van was a learning experience for all concerned.

Despite so much new terrain, each one of my family members managed to be gracious about what must have seemed like an array of annoying and difficult obstacles. The bulk of the work fell to my mother, sister, and grandmother. My dad and my brother were both working full-time, but would help out whenever they could. My godmother, who is a retired nurse, was also going to contribute. I needed help around the clock. I could do *nothing*. It's very, very strange to have to rely on others for everything. It took me a long time to get used to giving "orders." In those early days I was acutely conscious of seeming to tell anyone what to do. But the fact was, I had no choice. If I needed something, someone had to get it for me. I needed to get on the wait list for therapy at Burke hospital, I needed to figure out which wheelchair I wanted to replace the chair I was currently renting, I wanted to begin to find out about new surgeries and research studies. I couldn't even dial a number and make a phone call without help. Everything took so much longer and required so much focus and energy to accomplish, that by the third day at home, I was questioning whether it was worth getting out of bed at all.

My sister reminded me that this wasn't an option. "Checco," she said gently, "c'mon. We've got to get you up at some point."

Despite her insistence that I keep getting out of bed in the morning, those early months after my accident were hard. I laid low. I didn't want to be around others, even old friends. Mentally, I made the excuse that I was too busy. I had to order a wheelchair. I had to do therapy. I had to find out if we could get our own van with a ramp. I was constantly trying to figure out how my insurance was going to cover everything. I was researching experimental trials and surgeries. There was so much to do and to learn, that it just didn't feel appropriate to hang out with a friend, because I had all these new responsibilities on my shoulders. Although I continued to meet with Suzan once a week to practice breathing and meditation, the only other people I saw on a regular basis were the members of my family.

Bottom line, I didn't want people to see me like this. I was extremely uncomfortable being in public or in a social setting. If my parents noticed this reluctance, they must have decided it was in my best interests to expand my horizons. Every Sunday, they would insist on some kind of outing. Usually, we'd go to a local restaurant. Other times, we'd venture farther. I understood that it was important to keep up these excursions—to make this statement that we were going to continue to do things together as a family—but in those early days, as soon as we left the house I couldn't wait to get home again. Whenever we entered a restaurant, I was sure that all eyes turned in my direction. In fact, people were probably less interested in me than I thought, but I was so self-conscious at this time that any kind of attention was unwelcome. In my mind, I was still an able-bodied person who happened to be sitting in a wheelchair. I hated the idea that people might see me as a disabled person.

Since my injury, I had lost the neurological function that allowed me to feel most of my skin, and as a result I had stopped reacting to hot and cold in normal ways. The whole time I'd been in the ICU and at Mount Sinai, I didn't sweat as much as a drop. As a result, my pores had become clogged with toxins. I had acne, rosacea, dry flaking skin, you name it. My lips were chapped and raw. I felt that I looked monstrous. When we went out, my mother would try to persuade me to get dressed up, but I would refuse. Instead, I'd wear my hospital pants, and the same brown cotton long-sleeved shirt that I'd been wearing all week long. I didn't care how I looked, because I didn't want to stand out any more than I already did. When we'd arrive at the restaurant, I'd focus on getting to the table as soon as possible. I felt more comfortable when everyone else was sitting down, because at least we were all at the same level and I didn't feel like I stuck out. But then the food would arrive, and someone would have to spoon-feed me. I was twenty-four years old and getting fed by my mother in a restaurant.

Mostly, people would sort of half-glance in my direction, and that was it. But other times, complete strangers would seek more direct contact. "What happened to you?" was the classic question.

"I broke my neck," I would mumble.

"How did you do that?" they would want to know.

"I jumped in the shallow end of a pool."

One time, someone actually said to me: "You broke your neck in a pool?! That's a stupid way to break your neck!" *OK,* I thought, because there's a *good* way and a *bad* way to break your neck?

Some people would even grab and feel my arms, as if they wanted to see if I was real. One of my dad's patients was visiting our house one day and decided it would be a good idea to rub a Bible on my head. Someone in the street felt compelled to grab my cheeks. Another time, a stranger shook my wheelchair to see how sturdy it was. I had become public property.

It was hard to anticipate exactly how people were going to react. But what disturbed me the most was when people assumed that my physical disabilities were somehow a reflection of my intellectual abilities. One day, we were visiting the Metropolitan Museum of Art in Manhattan. This was one of our regular family outings: The museum was big enough so that we could spend an hour or two escaping the crowds. But this being the Clark family, the conversation soon turned to where we were going to have lunch. That day we chose to go to the Petrie Court café, a beautiful spot overlooking Central Park. After we found a table, the waiter came over to take our drink orders. As he reeled off the list of beverages, for some reason, he kept leaning in my direction and shouting really loudly. Maybe he thought I was deaf.

Then, when I ordered a dirty martini, he seemed completely bewildered.

"Are you allowed . . . I'm sorry . . ." He then turned toward my sister and parents and asked, "Is he allowed to drink?"

I tried to brush it off with a joke: "Oh, you mean, because I look so young and fresh? I get that a lot." What did I look like? A blubbering buffoon? I guess I could have used a haircut, but still.

When the waiter brought the martini over, my sister gestured in my direction and said, "He might need a bib."

Another time, we had gone out on a Sunday to a nearby café. My mother and I were in line when three little boys wearing Cub Scout uniforms came in with their mother. They were giggling and talking, but as soon as they saw me, they stopped dead in their tracks. One of the boys actually let his lollipop fall from his hand.

"Billy, Billy, c'mon," his mother called to him. Billy was blocking the entrance to the café, but he was oblivious to everything. He just couldn't stop staring at me. I had to smile. The poor child's mother was embarrassed beyond belief, and as she pulled on Billy's jacket to move him out of the way, he stepped on his lollipop and made a loud crunch. Billy's eyes were still fixed on my wheelchair.

The next time I looked around, I realized that Billy's brother was touching one of my wheels with one finger. I looked away, then I looked back. Every time I looked away, he would move his hand and touch some other part of the wheelchair. When he saw my face turned toward him, he wouldn't move; he was like a statue. I guess he thought if he stayed perfectly still, I wouldn't see him. Then he started grabbing the wheel of my chair.

"I think someone really likes your wheelchair," said my mom.

"Please stop," I pleaded with her, because now I'd started to giggle uncontrollably.

"I am *so* sorry . . . ," said the boy's mother, pulling on his shirtsleeve to drag him away from me. But the boy would not move. "C'mon. Just . . . *move*. Move!" Now everyone was looking at us.

"Oh, it's fine. He can touch my chair. I don't care," I said.

"Well, that's good, because he isn't budging," said someone else in line, which made everyone laugh. By now the boy's poor mother was red in the face with embarrassment. Eventually she picked him up and took him outside.

She needn't have felt bad. Actually, I understood the boy's reaction to my wheelchair. For him, it was like a cool new toy, he just wanted to touch it and see if it was real. His response had been direct and honest. I preferred this to the half-glances I usually got from the adults in the room. And so the family outings continued, even though all I really wanted was to vanish into thin air. I didn't want this new life. Somehow it was easier to pretend that nothing had changed if I stayed at home where no one could see me and remind me of the obvious.

Throughout this time, I was tortured by a thousand "what-ifs?" What if I had been able to do something to avoid my injury? What if I hadn't gone out to the beach that weekend? What if I'd never done the summer rental? What if I'd stayed in the city instead? What if I hadn't gone for that swim? What if I'd just gone to bed? There were so many alternative outcomes to that evening, so many different conclusions to the chain of events that had almost ended my life. And yet I hadn't died. Here I was, obsessively revisiting events, over and over again, always searching for an exit sign, some way of altering the outcome. Nothing helped. My thoughts revolved like abandoned luggage on a carousel, going exactly nowhere. I just knew I didn't want to be where I was. I didn't want this to be my story.

This became my major focus. How was I going to turn back the clock? How could I change the outcome so that everything could continue on track? Someone would have to figure out how to put this right. Until that happened, I just wanted to hibernate.

12

The Elephant in the Room

SOON AFTER RETURNING HOME, I BEGAN TO GO FOR THER-
apy at Burke Rehabilitation Hospital near my parents' home, the
same hospital where Christopher Reeve had gone after his injury. Here I repeated many of the basic exercises I had done at
Mount Sinai. I kept hoping things would get more challenging
next time I visited. Every few weeks I would be "evaluated." This
involved measuring how tight my muscles were, figuring out our
therapy goals, and setting a schedule for the work ahead. The
therapist filled out countless forms while taking my measure-
ments over and over, checking and rechecking to make sure everything was accurate. The reason for the evaluations was simple:
The therapist needed to document my present level of ability and
my subsequent progress for my insurance company so they could
assess if they wanted to continue paying for my treatment.

With my parents' support, I had also begun working with various private therapists at home. Three times a week I had a massage to help stimulate my circulation and stretch out my muscles
(my muscles would shiver because they were so tight and out of

use, and the massage helped them to relax). I went to the chiro-
practor to help realign my bones. I did acupressure, which helped
promote healing and offered pain relief (I don't like to take medication, so this was a good alternative). I worked for a while with
a hypnotherapist, doing positive meditations.

My family agreed that this kind of extra treatment was essential, but I knew it was also downright expensive. It seemed like
every therapist charged $150 a session, and it was all adding up.
Yes, my family is relatively well off, but in no way would I describe us as rich because, for my parents, working has always been
a necessity. Most nights during the week, my parents come home
at two a.m. after having dinner at the office because they have to
go through all the patients' medical charts and submit insurance
paperwork. Now they were working harder than ever and every
single dollar bill had to be counted, because we couldn't afford to
waste a cent anymore.

My bills just to live, even without doing any extra therapy or
treatments, were astronomical. For example, my sterile catheter
kits, which are a single-time use, cost $45 per day. Forty-five dol-
lars a day quickly adds up. Even so, all of my doctors and nurses
had told me the sterile catheter kits were mandatory to prevent
urinary tract infections and even bladder cancer. The kits themselves almost look like miniature surgical sets, coming complete
with sterile gloves, paper, a plastic bag with a long tube, and a
packet of iodine swabs. The only part that my insurance company
pays for, however, is the rubber tube I needed to urinate with, not
the kit itself.

"Where are they made?" I asked my mother.

"It says . . . hold on . . . Made in Mexico."

Money, for anyone who is disabled or sick, is one of those divid-
ing factors that can significantly affect your chances of recovery. If

I didn't have my family to care for me and sustain me financially, I would probably have had to go to a long-term nursing home facility, where I would be left in bed, all day, with a television on. No therapy, no hope, nothing.

I was also fortunate in that for the first two years after my injury—while I was still receiving ongoing coverage through COBRA—my insurance was great at paying my bills (catheter kits aside). Even so, there were so many other expenses that my parents were paying for out of pocket. My insurance didn't cover the ramp outside the house or the new shower my parents had put into a closet in the living room so I would be able to shower downstairs. It didn't cover the cost of a used van with a lift that we had bought so I could get around.

Even the treatments that were covered by insurance came with their own set of complications. One of the main differences between having a spinal-cord injury and other afflictions is that you become a patient for a much longer period of time. Therapy has to be a part of your day-to-day life, and so you become inherently accustomed to the pestering bureaucracies of the insurance reimbursement game. My mom was the one who dealt with claims at the doctor's office, and so she took on the task of handling all of my paperwork. Every little treatment I received had to be pre-approved, approved, evaluated, faxed, signed, and faxed again. There were so many calls and documents that it was an endless task, even for an expert like my mom. The giant folder that sat on her desk was growing ever bigger by the day.

Already, insurance was becoming an issue at Burke. On one particular day, I'd arrived for my usual session, but my physical therapist, George, seemed reluctant to get started.

"We need to discuss your therapy regimen," he said. I assumed we were finally going to talk about new approaches, some new technique he wanted to try. Instead, he wheeled me over to the table and pulled up my file.

"Francesco, when you first came here, we were seeing some progress, particularly with your fine motor skills." I nodded. I definitely credited my time at Burke with helping me to regain a degree of flexibility in my hands and fingers.

"But for the past few weeks, you seem to have plateaued," George went on. "You really haven't gotten any further with your rolling. When we did your evaluation last week, we had to report this. So now it's difficult for us to bill for your therapy sessions. If we can't show measurable improvement from week to week, with your type of injury, we can't get your sessions approved by the insurance company."

Rolling was an exercise we worked on constantly. It remains the most difficult thing for me to do, because you need the muscles of your entire body to achieve it. I knew I wasn't lazy, and that I had been trying as hard as I could. But now George seemed to be telling me that because I wasn't getting anywhere just yet, he was going to have to give up on me. I needed some clarification.

"Wait," I said. "So what you're telling me is that if I *don't* improve, I'll be kicked out?"

"Look, Francesco, I know this is hard, but there's only so much we can do for you. You should be really happy that you've made this much progress at all."

Happy that I'd made this much progress? No way was I done with therapy yet. I'd only been coming here for two months.

George was looking at me with an expression he must have thought was compassionate, but all I could see was pity, a reaction to my injury that I loathed.

"Francesco," George told me, "at some point, you're going to have to move on with your life." He didn't know how many times I'd already heard this speech. He seemed to have no idea how patronizing his words sounded. Move on with my life? Was he kidding me? Why don't *you* move out of my way, George, so that I can continue working hard on this injury that *I* have to live with!

I needed to point something out to him: "Didn't you just spend the past two months telling me how important it is to do therapy?" I asked.

The whole time I'd been at Burke, all I'd heard was that physical therapy was essential. So essential that I should only be doing it for two months? From what I'd heard, when many patients stopped their therapy, their muscles got so tight and their arms so weak that they quickly lost the little mobility that they did have. Everyone knew the horror stories about patients who couldn't even straighten their legs anymore because they'd been in a sitting position for so long that the muscles and tendons had hardened to the extent of contracture. The only way of reversing contracture is through surgery, at which point doctors and therapists say, "Well, that's what happens when you stop doing physical therapy. . . ."

"It's just that you've plateaued, Francesco," George repeated. "At this point, we can't be certain that you're going to make any measurable improvement going forward."

Wait a minute, how did he even know I had plateaued? Maybe I plateaued for a short period of time, but that didn't mean I was finished. I knew I had the ability to get more muscle return, but I would never have any chance of doing this if I didn't continue with therapy. What George was telling me was that my body wasn't healing fast enough, or more precisely, my body wasn't healing according to the insurance company's predetermined deadlines. It wouldn't be until I started meeting other patients who had been injured years before me that I would understand that this was an all too common experience, and that everyone with SCI comes up against this same fundamental obstacle.

When we got home that day, my mom and I called my insurance company to find out what was going on. By now, we were already on first-name terms with my caseworker, Lela, because we spoke to her on a weekly basis. In fact, we spoke to her more than I spoke to some of my oldest friends at this point in my life.

Right away, Lela told me that there was no reason for me to stop my therapy at Burke. Great. This was what I wanted to hear. My insurance company was more than willing to pay for me to continue with my physical therapy. So why was George telling me otherwise?

Then Lela asked how many hours of therapy I was doing each week. I told her I was doing forty-five minutes of physical therapy and forty-five minutes of occupational therapy.

"Francesco, you know, you could be doing more than that," she informed me.

It turned out that my insurance company would be happy to pay for three full hours of therapy a day—twice the amount I was currently receiving. Were they kidding me?

After we hung up, my first reaction was one of confusion. If I was eligible for more therapy, then why wasn't the hospital offering this to me? My second reaction was to feel furious. When I'd arrived at Burke, I'd assumed that the therapists' goal was to work with me, not to shrug me off because that was easier for *them*. After speaking to Lela, I became convinced that George really didn't care very much about my recovery. Maybe it was just that he didn't know what to do with me as the weeks went on. Maybe he didn't have much experience with spinal-cord injuries. Actually, I have come to realize that it was probably a little bit of both.

The next day, I spoke to George and told him about what the representative at my insurance company had told me.

He froze.

"You called your case manager at your insurance company?" I thought about all the other patients doing therapy around me. Was it possible that they were eligible for more therapy, and just didn't realize it? I'd noticed that the older patients in particular tended to accept whatever they were told by the hospital. It was like they didn't have the energy or the information to stick up for themselves.

"George," I said, "if you don't feel comfortable working with me, I'll happily change therapists. But I want to continue working here, and I want three hours of therapy a day." I didn't care if he was bored; I needed this therapy. If my insurance company was willing to pay, that's what I was going to get. Reluctantly, George agreed to continue with me a while longer.

Now he just had to figure out what to do with me for another hour and a half.

"I want to do more rolling practice," I informed him. "If I'm going to be discharged because I can't roll over, then I want rolling to be my focus." George had no choice but to follow my lead.

Insurance was the common thread in every interaction with my hospital therapists, and not only at Burke. When someone said the dreaded I-word, it was for a couple reasons: the therapist didn't want to work with me anymore and was using that as an excuse; the hospital wasn't making as much money from my treatment as they would from a newer patient; or I had become too demanding to work with, and the therapist just didn't know what to do with me. Often the therapists I encountered were young. Maybe I challenged them in ways that they simply couldn't handle. They had been taught that my injury was hopeless. They told me they could help me maintain the little mobility that I did have, but sometimes it seemed as if they weren't even prepared to do that.

I thought a lot about the TV special I had seen about Christopher Reeve—all the amazing, progressive therapy that he was doing every single day. This was so inspiring, but it almost made me feel more infuriated by my therapists, because the message that I got was that unless I was a celebrity, I might as well forget about getting better. Mr. Reeve could penetrate the prevailing complacency of the medical community and blow it to pieces, but I wondered if his doctors and therapists would be so eager to push the envelope if he weren't so famous. This way, if he made even the smallest improvement, they got the credit in the media. I could see why this would be appealing—any press a doctor gets for a research study means more recognition and validation from the medical community, more demand by participants, and more grant money—but even so, it was a tough pill to swallow.

Money was the elephant in every room. I was beginning to learn that instead of ignoring the subject of money, or tiptoeing around it, I was going to have to play the game, turning things to my advantage as best I could. While my goals remained the same, I had shifted gears. I needed to accept that being a patient means being a commodity and that, sadly, no one is going to help you out of the goodness of their own hearts. I couldn't assume that George's goal was my recovery, therefore I had to make sure that my goals were *my* priority, so I could keep strongly advocating for myself. I was determined to work every part of my body, my legs in particular. I began to set my own agenda, whether I was working at home or at the hospital, focusing on sitting balance one month, then rolling another month, then transferring from the chair to the mat the month after that. This way I could keep things fresh and give myself a sense of progression. I might not be famous, but even so, I had to find ways to make certain that the complacency of my therapists and the restrictions of insurance companies didn't control my recovery. I wanted to be the one to do that.

13

One Year On

OFTEN IN THAT FIRST YEAR PEOPLE ASKED ME, "ARE YOU angry as a result of the injury?" I would always give them the diplomatic answer: "No, I'm not. I'm too busy to be angry." But the truth of the matter was that I *was* angry. I was angry at people who made dumb comments; I was angry at therapists like George who wanted me to "move on with my life"; I was furious at the medical community who believed I was a lost cause; I was mad about the politics that were preventing stem-cell research; I was infuriated by the insurance game I was having to play in order to get treated. My parents raised me to be polite, so it wasn't like I was going to start shouting at every second person I met. But at this point, I hadn't figured out ways of channeling my anger and using it to propel me forward. On good days, the anger helped me to become productive and transform negative energy into positive action. On bad days, it settled inside me, making me feel helpless and sad.

A few days before the first anniversary of my accident, I hit a wall. My family and friends were aware that the anniversary was coming around and made sure to reach out to me that week, which was great, but it only served to remind me how much time had gone by. I couldn't believe it had been a year. I couldn't believe that it had been twelve months since I'd been able to get up from my seat, run up stairs, and open the door to my room. Many, many times I'd imagine the pleasure of picking up a pen and writing a note. Or going to shake someone's hand to say hello. Or getting blisters on my feet because I'd been hiking. Or waiting in line for forty-five minutes to get tickets for a bad movie. All the things I had taken for granted in the past—or even complained about—were a dream for me now.

At the time of my injury, I was barely out of college. There were so many things I hadn't done yet. I felt as if I had been cheated out of my life. My life was my injury now. I spent all my time in hospitals, thinking about insurance and money, worrying about things that no young person usually has to think about. I'd wanted to do well in the world, to make my parents proud, to make a contribution. Now everything I'd done before my injury felt irrelevant. I knew my injury had been an accident, but it still felt like I had let everyone down.

As the anniversary approached, I disappeared inside myself, trying to figure out what everything meant. Where was my value, now that I couldn't help myself, couldn't work or earn money, or survive a day without the support of my family? I just wanted to fix this. The guilt I felt about my family's sacrifice made me try harder at my therapy, but more than anything, I just wished I didn't have to put them through any of it. I kept fighting and I kept trying, but after a year, what did I have to show for all that effort? My life was on pause. My career was nonexistent. Even my college degree felt worthless to me now, because how was I ever going to use it? I didn't want to socialize, because I didn't want people to see me. I couldn't even think about the fact that no one would want to be in a relationship with me, because there was only so much I could deal with at this point. I just didn't have the brain energy to follow that train of thought. At least I'd been single at the time of my injury, and this was one thing, at least, that I didn't have to register as a loss.

Every night I lay in bed and ask myself the following questions: What did I do wrong? Why did this happen? There were no answers, because all I really wanted was to turn back the clock twelve months. I wanted to wake up in the morning in my old apartment, pull on some clothes, make myself a coffee, and sprint out the door to work. I wanted my job back, my social life, my entire existence. And because I couldn't have what I most wanted, I just kept asking the same questions over and over again. Sometimes my hectic therapy schedule distracted me from my problems and kept me focused. But at other times I felt as if therapy was taking over everything. I would drive to Burke in the morning and do three hours of therapy. Upon arriving home, I did another hour and thirty minutes of therapy. Most days, I wound up exhausted. All I could do was hope that I was actually making progress.

The anniversary underlined for me that as hard as I worked, I was still trapped in this situation, and seemingly unable to change it. No matter how much my family tried to help, the simple fact remained: if I was lying in bed feeling thirsty and there was a glass of water on the nightstand not even an arm's length away, I couldn't reach for it to take a drink.

The week of the anniversary, my friend Suzan and I met for our regular meditation session. Afterward, we ate some home-cooked Italian food together. It was always such a pleasure for me to see her. We had always gotten along, and since my accident, we had grown even closer. That week, I told Suzan how depressed I felt at the prospect of a year gone by.

"It's hard," I told her. "It's making me reflect on everything, and not in a good way. I just want to have something to show for this year except for this wheelchair."

"You know, I actually *like* that it's your anniversary," said Suzan, without skipping a beat.

"Are you serious?" I asked her. "Why?"

"Because it reminds me that you're alive," she replied. "That you didn't die. I'm so grateful that you're here today to talk about it with me."

"I guess, I never—"

"No," she said. "You just keep working a little more every day. That's what makes a difference."

I knew she was right. I nearly died that day in the pool and even with everything I was going through now, I knew I was grateful I had survived.

With Suzan's help, we began going over the small milestones of the past year. I was stronger. I was able to hold my head up with the brace. I was figuring out a way to use a regular fork to feed myself. I could just about hold a phone, even if I couldn't dial a number. I was at a point where I could read a book alone. I could sit up at the edge of my bed. All of these were things that were impossible for me immediately after the injury.

"Holy cow, Francesco!" Suzan pointed out. "You're unstoppable!"

I had spent a whole year asking myself, "Why did this happen to me?" but I had asked the question so many times that it had begun to wear itself out. It had worn *me* out. I knew in my heart there was no point in asking "why me?" anymore. I just had to grow up and begin answering the big questions that everyone has to confront at some point in life. For some people, it takes losing a parent or a loved one before they start to think, Why did I get dealt these cards? Where do I go from here? What's the purpose of my time here? It was just that my accident was forcing me to wise up at a very young age.

I was realizing there was no way to go back in time. Suzan was right. I just had to find a way to inch myself forward.

Part Two

THE NEXT STEP

14

Hey, Look Who's Walking!

WHEN YOU'VE BEEN DEPRIVED OF THE ABILITY TO WALK, THE whole *idea* of walking becomes intoxicating to you. You dream about walking. Your biggest fantasy involves getting up out of your chair and going to fix yourself a sandwich in the kitchen. There were days when I would have given anything—truly anything—just to leave the house to run an errand. I even missed standing in line at Starbucks.

One year after my injury, I was beginning to worry that I might forget what it felt like to walk altogether, and this added further fuel to my determination to participate in the treadmill study I knew was taking place at the Kessler Foundation Research Center. At Kessler, I would be able to walk on a treadmill while supported by a harness and a team of therapists, just as I had seen Christopher Reeve do on T V. The treadmill approach made perfect sense to me: if you want to learn to walk again, you needed to practice actually *walking*. But the abiding attitude of the doctors and therapists I had met until now was that if you couldn't feel a part of your body, then it wasn't worth working it. This seemed counterintuitive to me. I felt that I *should* be working my legs to help stimulate recovery and healing. I wanted to be on my feet. I wanted to be mobile again. I knew that if nothing else, being in motion would have a beneficial effect on my circulation, my muscles, and my bones.

As it turned out, Kessler was about an hour and a half from my parents' house, but to be honest, even if it had been in Antarctica, I would have found a way to get there. At the beginning of 2003, I got the call from Kessler to say they needed people for the treadmill study and would definitely consider me. I then began a rigorous evaluation process to see if I was strong enough to withstand the strenuous workout of the treadmill. Many people with spinal-cord injuries suffer from osteoporosis, the bone disease caused by lack of minerals. When you injure your spinal cord, your metabolism immediately changes: You start rapidly losing the minerals in your body, calcium in particular, which weakens your bones. The problem is compounded by the fact that you're not putting weight on your legs, making them weaker still. I just had to hope that because I was relatively young and my injury was new, this wouldn't be too much of a factor.

Happily, I passed the tests and at Kessler I found myself surrounded by people who loved what they were doing and wanted to break new ground. Dr. Rose, the doctor in charge of the trials, and her research assistants were all incredibly enthusiastic and energetic. Right away, I felt I was in safe hands. These were people who were pushing the boundaries of conventional thinking about spinal-cord injuries and I knew I wanted to do whatever I could to help them.

The first time I saw the huge treadmill device, I recognized it immediately as the one I'd seen Christopher Reeve using. There was a pneumatic metallic arm hovering above the treadmill belt, and various cords and carabiners hanging from a hoist.

The treadmill seemed of mammoth proportions, and it had metallic posts on the back corners of it. The six air tanks looked like the ones people would use when scuba diving, except these were four or five times bigger. There was a computer desk to the right of the treadmill, as well as another desk in the back of the room. All of this was housed in a very small room that made the equipment seem even bigger.

"Basically, the way the body-weight-supported treadmill works is, we strap you into a parachute harness and hook you into a crane which can lift you onto the treadmill," Steven, one of the assistants in the study, informed me. "Our goal is to have you do twenty-minute walking bouts. Of course, that is something we'll gradually work toward, so it won't be such a shock to you."

"So, how will I walk?" I felt like I was asking an obvious question, but it hadn't been addressed, and I was trying to connect the dots. Why the air tanks? What about the various monitors? Apart from anything else, I couldn't figure out how I was going to get up from my wheelchair and into the walking position.

"There will be two of us guiding your legs," Dr. Rose explained. "And I'll be guiding your hips to make sure your body mechanics are working properly and in symmetric rhythm. The crane will be programmed to hold up the minimum amount of weight possible. We also will be guiding your legs less and less each time we do this."

But first I had to get into the parachute harness. The team lifted me out of my chair so that I could be stretched out horizontally on a therapy mat.

"We have to strap you in pretty tight," Dr. Rose explained, "or your body could slip out of it and your walking will be affected by the poor positioning."

I was already hooked up to various electrodes, sensors, a heart monitor, and blood-pressure cuffs. Infrared cameras were going to be taking images of my body as I moved, which would later be reconstructed on the computer in three dimensions. There were about five belts to tighten, readjust, and retighten on the harness. Pretty soon, I was strapped in so tight it was difficult to breathe. Sitting made the harness feel even tighter. My midsection was now stiff and almost immovable, with what felt like a metal girdle restraining it.

Next I was wheeled up the long wooden ramp that led up to the base of the treadmill. The first time, this was intimidating, exciting, and overwhelming all at once.

"We're going to lock you into the lift now," said Steven.

Large metal hooks were fastened around my straps with loud clicks. I was now attached to the pneumatic crane by a series of cables. One of the other assistants, Philip, started a program on the computer next to the treadmill that controlled the lift. With a loud *pfft!* the hooks shot up into the air, pulling the harness straps I was wearing along with them. The sound was startling at first, only because the lifting mechanism looked big enough to lift a small car. Thankfully, it only tugged a little at my body.

"OK. Ready when you are, Dr. Rose," said Philip.

"Francesco, we're going to increase the pressure in the airlift to pull your body and help you stand above the treadmill for a moment. When you are up, we will take away your wheelchair and replace it with a regular office chair, which you will sit back down on. That's when you will be hooked up to the mask, and we'll finish applying all the leads."

I heard the air pump filling the piston with air and as it did, the machine began to lift me up. My body was lifted quickly and effortlessly. I felt the tug on my chest and shoulders minimize a bit, and before I knew it, I was standing.

"What happens is that over time, the harness is going to support less and less of your body weight," Dr. Rose explained. "It should start to feel more like normal walking rather than how you're feeling right now. You probably feel like you're suspended from the ceiling." She was right. My feet didn't feel like they were holding me up, the harness did.

After I had been hoisted into the air, Dr. Rose strapped a breathing mask around my mouth and nose. She used what looked like Silly Putty to seal the mask to my face.

"This is to prevent any air from entering or escaping the mask . . . which measures the amount of oxygen you breathe into and out of your lungs."

Now that the mask was on, they were going to start up the treadmill so that I could begin to walk. I had no idea how this would feel. It had been over a year since I'd taken as much as a step. Right away, my height was working against me. Even just to remain standing, there was a lot of weight to control and balance. Dr. Rose had hold of my hips, two other assistants were going to help guide my legs, and someone else was at the computer operating the machinery. Dr. Rose gave the go-ahead and the treadmill started to slowly, slowly move. I had no idea what to do. The harness was holding up so much of my weight that it felt like my feet were lightly tapping on the treadmill, but I couldn't be sure. It didn't feel like I was walking. It felt more like I was floating.

My mom was there, cheering me on, but I was so focused on trying to stay upright that I couldn't even look at her.

Dr. Rose called out: "Left, right, left, right, left, right . . ." and told me to do the same. This way, the two assistants on each leg would be in sync with my intentions. As they began to move my legs to match the pace of the treadmill, I rocked immediately and violently to the left. It was almost impossible to get everything balanced. My upper and lower body were refusing to work in sync with each other. I had spent so long seated and lying down that the muscles in my legs were unbelievably tight. To make matters worse, various muscles in my legs, abdominals, and back began activating and firing from lack of use. My legs would kick out involuntarily, and this would yank me off balance again. It was incredibly challenging for me to remain upright. It took four therapists and an insane amount of concentration to keep my body in the correct alignment and establish any momentum. You could hear in the tone of our voices the tension we all felt. The small room quickly got very hot, all of us sweating from the hard work. During that first session, I was so focused on trying to balance my walking pattern that I hadn't noticed my left ear was repeatedly hitting the metal carabiner until it bled.

Despite the challenges, this was what I had committed to do, and I was determined to get better at it. Three days a week I would go to Kessler and work for three hours a day. My mom would drive me, a journey which could last as long as two hours if there was traffic. It took almost the whole day to get there and back, and do my sessions there. Even so, being in such a stimulating setting was inspiring. Here were people in the scientific community who wanted to *prove* that spinal-cord injuries were reversible. At Kessler, I didn't feel like a lost cause; I felt like I was playing my part in providing valuable data in a seriously under-researched field. Because so many doctors had spent so many years assuming that there was nothing anyone could do about spinal-cord injuries, Dr. Rose was navigating uncharted territory.

After the treadmill sessions I was exhausted and I was starving. The walking took so much out of me, I ate two cheeseburgers at a single sitting. Once I was done eating, it was on to physical therapy. My therapist, Ken, was in constant discussions with Dr. Rose about what I had been doing in the treadmill sessions. Ken was a PhD, but he also had a degree in physical therapy and had been an athlete most of his life. He knew I liked to exert myself and he understood the type of challenging workout I needed. Finally, here was someone who wanted to do more than transfer me from the wheelchair to the workout mat. Even so, Ken could see that I wasn't yet strong enough to physically move all of my own body weight, so he started making me lift light weights placed on my wrists to strengthen my arms. This was going to help my balance while treadmill walking and I could feel myself getting stronger with every session.

During my final evaluation many months later, Dr. Rose showed me videos of my early sessions to remind me of how far I'd come. The first videos showed me being held in position by my doctor and her assistants while my upper body rocked violently from side to side. I was completely disjointed. In the later videos, the team was barely doing any pulling and lifting. Instead, they were just helping to guide my legs. It looked pretty smooth. I was perfectly balanced; I was even swinging my arms to stay in step. Dr. Rose showed me several graphs and charts she had put together using the data from the tests I'd undergone after I'd finished participating in the study. She told me that they were going to use my results for the research papers they planned to publish about the treadmill training.

"Your data was one of the best any of the research facilities has obtained," she told me. "Ever."

I couldn't wait to tell my parents this.

"What we found through the surface EMG electrode readings on your leg muscles is that your legs are showing activity with each step, just like they're supposed to," Dr. Rose continued. "Also, your lung capacity is now better than that of an average person and your heart rate is what people call 'runner's heart' because it beats so slowly, which is good."

As she continued talking, she was growing increasingly animated with every new chart. I felt like this was a doctor who was genuinely optimistic and encouraging about my situation, who believed I could get better. I wanted to hug her.

"You'll be amazed by what we found after the bone- and muscle-density scan," she went on. "Your bone density is within normal limits, and your muscle mass has actually increased by seven pounds since you started the treadmill study."

What Dr. Rose was telling me was that I was getting better. I had actual proof I was getting better. This wasn't subjective observation. This was scientific fact, in writing, on video, in photos, and in charts. I had gone beyond the conventional therapy model, and I was getting results. I had worked so hard on my legs that they were stronger. Period. What's more, my days at Kessler left me burned out, in a good way. Usually my days were so sedentary, but the cardiovascular exercise of being on the treadmill brought on a major change in my mood. I felt much less anxious and jittery, I was more optimistic, calmer, and definitely more energetic. Unlike the sorely limited regimen I'd been on up to this point, the sheer effort of walking on the treadmill made me feel more physically capable, more alive—more me.

But even with all the good news, there was still a big part of me that wanted to ask Dr. Rose: "If I'm making so much progress, why am I still in a wheelchair?" I wanted something to show for all my hard work besides the graphs and charts. I wished I could go and see my friends and have them say "Wow! You really did get better." Maybe Dr. Rose could give me a medal, but even so, I wanted my hard work to be shown not only on my sleeve, but preferably on my legs. I wanted to be independent. I wanted to be functional. I wasn't there yet. I was making progress; I just wanted to make more progress.

A Doctor's Son

"YOU SHOULD START A RESTAURANT," MY BROTHER MIKE tells my mother. We're all gathered around the family dining table one Thursday night—family night—feasting on *crescentina,* little light and crusty pieces of fried dough filled with cheese that melt on the tongue. "There's an empty spot where the bank used to be."

"No way!" my sister interrupts. "Could you imagine cooking all day, every day? And for people you don't even know?"

"I would do it," my mother muses. "If three friends did it with me. We could take certain days and cook only on those days." I can see my mother starting to make the calculations.

"If you had help, it would do really well," adds Valerie, my brother's wife. By now, she is perfectly accustomed to every Northern Italian dish on the table, a succession of mouthwatering antipasti.

"Seriously? She's already so busy as it is!" I point out. Everyone knows that it would be impossible, but still, we're enjoying indulging the fantasy. A restaurant serving my mother's and grandmother's food would be a huge success.

My mother disappears into the kitchen and returns with the tagliatelle. My father's eyes grow wide at the sight of the steaming pasta. Like him, we're all hungry.

Ring, ring! The phone interrupts, as usual. Dad ducks his head down, avoiding the inevitable. My mom goes to answer the phone.

"Yes, he's right here. One minute . . ."

For as long as I can remember, my dad has been getting calls from his patients at all hours of the day and night. This evening is no exception.

"Always during dinner," my father grumbles. "I just sat down. Sheesh."

But as he picks up the phone, his tone changes: He sounds warm, concerned, and above all, calm.

"Hello, Dr. Clark speaking . . . yes . . . she . . . what? She . . . no, that's too high. I'll be right there."

As he goes to hang up the phone, my mother hands him hot bread with Brie on it. "Eat this," she says. "I'll have fish ready for you when you come back. *Ciao!*" She rubs his bald head and kisses his cheek.

Many dinners have been sacrificed over the years, but still, my father keeps up his house calls. There are very few doctors who provide such an old-fashioned service anymore, but my dad won't give it up because he believes that when he sees patients directly, he can treat them more effectively. That's why he got into medicine in the first place—because he wanted to help people feel better. It doesn't matter that he misses dinner. The most important thing is that he is there when someone needs him.

For my dad, being a doctor isn't just his job; it's his calling. It's also the reason he met my mother. After finishing his undergraduate degree at Manhattan College, he decided to go to the University of Bologna in Italy to study medicine. One day, he was in the university's Johns Hopkins library when a striking young

Italian woman came over to him and asked him to stop rustling his newspaper so loudly. This was my mother. She had been born in Bologna and grew up there, and that day, she was working on her doctoral dissertation in languages at the library. My mother says that the moment she told my father to shut up was the moment she knew she would marry him.

On one of their early dates, my father arrived on his bicycle; my mother in her Fiat Cinquecento—those tiny little cars you see wherever you go in Italy. My dad was so distracted at the prospect of seeing my mother that his bike collided with the Cinquecento. The rest of the date was spent at the local emergency room—an appropriate setting for a future doctor and his wife, although not the most romantic of venues. When my mother's parents came to collect them both from the hospital, this was the first time they'd met their daughter's new boyfriend, complete with shorts that were ripped and bloody from the accident. If they didn't think much of this disheveled American on first meeting, they soon realized that he was an excellent match for their daughter. My father is characteristically quiet and collected, very calm and strong. My mother is the talker, the spitfire who motivates him to forge ahead. Soon they decided to get married.

After they had both finished their studies in Bologna, they continued to live in Italy, where my older brother was born. By the time I came along, they had moved back to the United States so my dad could begin his practice. From the start, my dad took somewhat of an unconventional approach to treating his patients. He had studied in Europe, where doctors are more open to alternative therapies such as homeopathy, vitamins, and herbal remedies. From the beginning, he was overly cautious about prescribing them antibiotics, which he felt would lessen the body's natural immunity. Today, this is common thinking, but back in the 1970s when my dad was starting out, he was definitely a pioneer. Soon my mom stepped in, helping my dad with the administrative side of his business, organizing the office, and settling the accounts. She went back to school, training as a dietician and phlebotomist, so she could help create the nutritional plans and do the blood work for the patients.

Word started to get around that my parents were having some success helping people who were facing fatal and debilitative illnesses. My father found he could improve the quality of life of patients who were undergoing chemotherapy or patients who had Lyme disease, chronic fatigue, diabetes, high blood pressure, or arthritis, by combining conventional and complementary medicine to get the best results. He discovered that when the patient and doctor work together in a proactive manner, amazing things can happen. One woman he worked with, who had been diagnosed with six months to live, went on to live more than six years.

Although I often felt as if the majority of the medical profession had tossed me on the scrap heap, my parents never made me feel that way. When it came to my recovery, their goal for me was that I should be able to get back as much function as possible. If I read something about a research trial that was going on, my dad read all the literature associated with it and then sat with me, taking the time to explain it in detail, so I had a fuller understanding of what was involved. He never used the word "never" around me. He was always open to the idea that we could find out more and that the prevailing opinion of the doctors we encountered could be proven wrong. Thanks to him and to my mom, it was second nature for me to take an imaginative and proactive approach to my recovery.

There was no doubt that I was in an imperfect situation. I was paralyzed, living at home with my parents, with no prospects of being able to work or carve out my own path in the world. It was like someone had hit a giant Pause button on my life. I'm not going to say I was happy about this. But one thing I never questioned was that I was in the right environment for my recovery. I had people who cared for me, who were rallying around and making enormous sacrifices on my behalf, without complaint. I had my brother and sister to help me and crack jokes at my expense. I had my grandmother to help care for me. I had a mother who was the world's greatest cook and my best advocate, and a father whose calm optimism and expertise was inspiring me to keep pushing forward, no matter how difficult it seemed at times.

As the months went by, I found I needed them more than ever. In many ways, it became harder to deal with my situation, not easier. That first year, the shock of what had happened to me shielded me from reality. It was impossible to believe that my injury was real. I would wake up in the morning and expect to discover that this was all a bad dream. But by the second year, it was getting harder to kid myself. The reality was sinking in. This wasn't a bad dream. There were no quick fixes. I was making some progress, but I was going to have to be extremely patient and strong-willed. Many people who sustain spinal-cord injuries suffer from depression, not surprisingly. I had weeks when I'd be gripped by an underlying sadness that was very hard to shake. This sadness was so powerful, it immobilized me beyond even my physical limitations. I would become frozen emotionally. When you're in this situation, you can start to have irrational thoughts. Some people start to think about suicide. It can be extremely challenging to find the will to continue when the prospects of progress are so limited.

Intuitively, my family understood the best way to lift my spirits was to keep making plans. We were always figuring out "the next step." While I continued to go to Kessler for the treadmill study, we were all aware that the study would come to an end and that we needed to have our eyes open for something else. This is what kept us going. Figuring out what came next. This is why I dispute, and will always dispute, the theory that doctors should discourage spinal-cord injury patients from being proactive and having hope. I think my family's positive attitude helped all of us, giving us something else to focus on beyond the considerable challenges of the everyday. Hope is still what keeps us ticking.

16

The Reeve Effect

IN NOVEMBER 2003, I READ AN ARTICLE THAT CHANGED MY life. It was the end of a long day of therapy at Kessler and I was lying in bed, reading a copy of *The New Yorker*. By now, I had enough control of my fingers to turn the pages of a magazine unaided. This was a major breakthrough, one that allowed me a small but valuable degree of independence. Reading a magazine in bed was a huge pleasure because for so long it had been impossible to do this without someone there to help. I was also learning to use the computer keyboard, using special hand splints that enabled me to tap with sticks on either palm, which was opening up a whole world to me.

That evening, I was flipping through the various sections when I caught a glimpse of the following headline: THE REEVE EFFECT.

It was subtitled, Can an Actor's Determination to Walk Again Change the Way Medical Research Is Conducted?

Immediately, I was hooked. I started reading the main article. I couldn't stop. When I got to the end, I went back to the beginning and started all over again.

The article spoke about Christopher Reeve's injury, how he had been told by his doctors that he would no longer be able to feel sensation in 90 percent of his body, and how since his accident, he had been forced to breathe with the help of a ventilator. The article also described the progress he'd made since then. He could move the toes on his left foot; he had some mobility in his legs when lying on his back and when exercising in a swimming pool. He was now able to feel his arms. His bone density was in the range of a normal adult, and his muscle strength was at around 80 percent—extraordinary for someone in a wheelchair. Mr. Reeve fully believed that one day he would get up out of his wheelchair and walk again. He had been accused of "being in denial" and giving people "false hope," but the fact remained that he had already defied the odds. The article stated that his improvements had been so encouraging that the medical community was rethinking the assumption that long-term paralysis was irreversible.

Christopher Reeve was effectively smashing through the complacencies and prevailing pessimism of the way the medical profession thinks about spinal-cord injuries.

"I was told from the very start that it was hopeless," Mr. Reeve told the reporter, "that it was impossible for me to regain movement below the shoulders. But every scientist should remove the word 'impossible' from his lexicon."

The article described how most doctors had simply stopped asking questions about spinal-cord injuries. Everyone believed SCI was incurable, therefore no one was doing research, therefore very little was actually known about the problem. Mr. Reeve was seeking out doctors who were prepared to go beyond the limited outlook of most in the medical profession. V. R. Edgerton, a neuroscientist at UCLA, had already begun looking into the effectiveness of body-weight-support therapy on animals with injured spinal cords. He worked with cats that had damaged cords, suspending them on a treadmill and moving their feet in a walking pattern. By the end of six months, most of the cats who had been using the treadmill began to regain their ability to walk. What Dr. Edgerton surmised from his study was that it was certain kinds of repetitive activity that held the key to the cats' recovery. When the cats were taught only to stand up, that's all they could do. But when they were trained to move their feet in a walking motion, they began to walk.

The article also spoke about another scientist, Dr. John McDonald, at Washington University in St. Louis. Dr. McDonald was also working with electrical-stimulation bikes, which use electrodes to fire paralyzed muscles into turning the wheels. When paralyzed patients used the electrical-stimulation bike on a regular basis, Dr. McDonald found they had fewer pressure sores, fewer blood clots, and fewer infections than those in the control group. This is extremely important when you're in a wheelchair, because when you're sitting all day, not only do you lose muscle and bone density, your skin can also start to break down, often leading to infections. The bike was helping to counteract all of these problems.

What impressed me most about the article was that it conveyed Mr. Reeve's sheer determination and impatience to take the next step. When research scientists would tell him, "It's going to take ten years," he would say, "Well, do it in five, because I can't wait that long." He was relentlessly pushing to end the restrictions on federal funding of human embryonic stem-cell research. These restrictions had been in place since 2001 when President George W. Bush banned funding for this kind of research unless the stem cells had been harvested prior to the ruling. The article spoke about a researcher named Hans Keirstead who was using existing stem-cell lines to create glial cells, which are known to support spinal-cord nerves. Dr. Keirstead had implanted glial cells in the backs of rats whose spinal cords had been crushed. He was getting impressive results. The rats with glial cells in their spines began to stand up and even take steps.

In the final part of the article, the reporter wrote about a Chinese neurosurgeon named Dr. Hongyun Huang, who had taken stem-cell research one step further: He was conducting stem-cell trials on humans. Working from a hospital in Beijing, Dr. Huang had inserted a type of stem cell called olfactory ensheathing cells into the spinal cords of nearly four hundred paralyzed patients. Although many in the spinal-cord-injury community felt Dr. Huang was moving way too fast, a researcher from the United States who had gone to Beijing to observe Dr. Huang's work reported back that his patients were regaining a degree of sensation and motor function. Three Americans had participated in the experimental procedures already. The moment I read about the surgery, I knew I had to know more.

That night, I looked up Dr. Huang's e-mail address online and started writing him an e-mail. I told Dr. Huang my story, how I was injured, my age, my level of injury. Just before hitting Send, I thought, "Here goes nothing."

That morning, at breakfast, I told my family about "The Reeve Effect." I told them about Dr. Huang, and how I thought I wanted to go to China to try his surgery. If my family had any reservations, they didn't speak of them. I think they were probably relieved that I had found what was next for my recovery. My mother and my sister immediately offered to come with me. The next morning, I checked my e-mail to see if Dr. Huang had replied. I felt like a little kid looking under the Christmas tree for presents on Christmas morning. "Don't get your hopes up. I'm sure he's busy," I thought to myself.

But instead, in bold black letters, I saw an e-mail from Dr.

Huang sitting in my inbox. His response was short and to the point; he asked me to send him a disk of the latest MRI of my injured spine and some other information. He wrote that the waiting list would be approximately six months. "No, no!" I said to myself, as I started to bang out my reply.

I explained that as my mother and sister would be accompanying me, we would need to come during the summer, during Charlotte's break. Then I clicked Send. As my mom walked into the room to wheel me down the ramp to the van, I barraged her with my news. The entire van ride to Kessler, I was jubilant. All right! So maybe this was what was next.

17

Learning to Stand My Ground

ALTHOUGH I WAS EXCITED ABOUT CHINA, I KNEW I NEEDED to find out everything there was to know about the surgery before fully committing to the trip. What exactly did the surgery entail? What was Dr. Huang's success rate and what progress could I expect to see afterward? How long was it going to take me to recover? Then there was the big question: How much was this going to cost? How much was the surgery itself? How much for airfares? There was the fact that my mom wasn't going to be able to work while she was away with me. We quickly figured out that my China trip was going to cost tens of thousands of dollars—and in the past eighteen months since my accident, I'd earned exactly nothing. My parents were determined that money wouldn't be a factor in the decision. Whatever the financial sacrifice to them, they would find a way to fund the surgery if that's what I decided I wanted to do. I knew how lucky I was.

"If you're able to do more and be more independent after the surgery," my mother insisted, "then it's going to be worth it."

"I know it's important to you," my dad told me. "And we all

want to do everything we can to support your decision. Your brother and sister agree."

My heart pounded just thinking about all the bills for the trip. I knew I needed to find out everything there was to know about Dr. Huang before signing up for the surgery. I needed to show my family that I was responsible. I couldn't afford to make any more mistakes. Dr. Huang had put me on a waiting list, and although initially I was frustrated that I wouldn't be able to have the surgery right away, I soon realized that I had been given a window of opportunity to do some real research. After my experience in the ICU, I didn't take lightly the idea of putting myself in the hands of another surgeon. I only wanted to do this if I could find out exactly what was involved. Finding out more proved to be challenging, however. Dr. Huang had only recently begun to perform these operations. He had published one article in English in March of 2003, eight months previously. Most of the evidence available was anecdotal. In fact, the reporter who had written the article on Christopher Reeve was the first journalist in the West to report on Dr. Huang. It was no wonder I hadn't read about him anywhere else.

By looking online, I discovered that Dr. Huang had been a doctoral student under one of the foremost SCI researchers in America, Dr. Wise Young at Rutgers University. This information made me feel a whole lot more confident about Dr. Huang's track record. Both doctors had conducted studies on rats with broken spinal cords in which the rats were injected with glial cells and began to regain function. After working with Dr. Young for several years, Dr. Huang went back to Beijing, where he began inserting glial cells into the spines of human patients. By the time he published his paper in 2003, he had performed surgery on 171 patients who were severely paralyzed. People previously unable to move hands or toes, perform bladder or bowel functions easily, were actually showing improvements in sensation and movement.

I spent a lot of time online, trying to figure it all out. My father reviewed everything I read about the surgery, combing through the fine print to make sure we knew exactly the risks and the chances of success. I came across the CareCure website, one of the leading websites for people with spinal-cord injuries, founded by Dr. Young—the same doctor whom Dr. Huang had worked under at Rutgers University. At that time, CareCure was hosting a blog written by Bob Smith, the first American to undergo Dr. Huang's surgery. Mr. Smith had been injured in a car accident in 1999. He was forty-seven years old and paralyzed from the neck down. I read every word of his descriptions about the surgery itself, the Chinese hospital, his recovery period. I learned some pretty important information: I would need to stay in Beijing for six weeks; I was going to have to bring my own medical supplies with me, as the hospital did not provide those; I needed to bring caregivers, because the Chinese nurses only provided patients with minimal care; and it would take me as long as two weeks to recover from the surgery. In the coming months, I continued to follow Mr. Smith's progress. After China, he went immediately to the Rehabilitation Institute of Michigan, where he continued to do intensive physical therapy, as mandated by Dr. Huang. Since his surgery, he was feeling stronger. His bladder function was improved, and he was even getting some sensation back in his hands and toes. This was enough for me. I knew if I saw that kind of improvement after surgery, I would be happy.

I decided to go to an open house at the W. M. Keck Center for Collaborative Neuroscience at Rutgers University in New Jersey. This was the center that was home to the Spinal Cord Injury Project led by Dr. Wise Young. Dr. Young remains at the forefront of finding a cure for spinal-cord injuries here in the United

States. After touring the lab, he gave a presentation and discussion about SCI research going on around the world. We saw charts and graphs and photographs of every major finding and breakthrough in the field. Although Dr. Young was careful not to name names, he warned us to beware of doctors who were taking advantage of the desperation that many patients feel after sustaining spinal-cord injuries. He went on to describe six specific doctors, all of whom were working on a cure and whose findings he did want to share with us. One of these was Dr. Huang.

"Most patients have recovered several levels of sensation and up to two levels of motor function after having undergone his procedure," Dr. Young said of Dr. Huang's work. "Remember that this data was taken from the first patients who underwent his surgery, and they are still recovering."

This was all that I needed to hear. These people were getting better; they were feeling and moving parts of their bodies they hadn't moved for years. And this was only the beginning. The surgery had yet to be perfected. The patients still had to do more intensive physical therapy.

"It's also important to realize that these are not complete cures—yet," Dr. Young continued. "We believe these are the first or second phases towards achieving a cure. We need these steps because they help to teach us what works and what doesn't work. When we understand that, then we can improve on these techniques with various combination therapies."

This I understood. Dr. Huang's research was a work in progress. I got that.

"You must keep in mind that there are really no randomized clinical trials for any of the current neurosurgical procedures," Dr. Young reminded us. "The big debate right now is, What is the level of evidence that's necessary and sufficient to take something to clinical trial?"

I had to ask him the million-dollar question: "Would you rec-
ommend that patients undergo these experimental procedures?"

"My official recommendation to patients is that they should
wait," said Dr. Young. "But many of them ignore me; they go on
ahead to do it anyway."   .

After we left, Charlotte asked me how I felt about what I'd
heard.

"I don't know," I told her. "I guess I feel confused and really
excited at the same time."

"I can understand that," she said. "But you heard it from one
of the leaders in the SCI field. Dr. Huang's patients are getting
better. There's no getting around that."

"What Dr. Young was saying was that it has to be the patient's
decision to sign up for surgery, right?"

"Right."

"So I'm going to China?"

"Of course you are," she said.

As I began to tell people about my plans, I got a variety of responses from them, ranging from positive to negative to downright misinformed. One day at Kessler, as I was getting strapped
into the harness to do my treadmill walking, I told Philip, one of
the research assistants, that I'd decided to go to China for the
surgery.

"But none of it is scientifically proven!" he immediately protested. "Dr. Huang can't show any real results yet. Nothing he's
doing has been backed by any third party or peer publication!"

"Kind of like any new research study in the beginning," I
pointed out. "Dr. Huang only just got started. He's using the techniques that have been performed on rats, and that data has been
studied and evaluated *in the United States.*" To be honest, I was sur-
prised that Philip of all people was so opposed to this. If anyone
should be interested in experimental procedures, then it should

be someone who is working in the same field. But Philip seemed determined to throw cold water on Dr. Huang's work.

"I just don't know, Francesco," he continued. "I think there's a strong possibility that you could go all that way and spend all that money on something that's basically a placebo effect."

"OK. But would the placebo effect explain why patients are getting back motor function?" I asked. "Don't you want to know more about that? If you were paralyzed, wouldn't you want to do whatever it takes to get better and play your part in the search for a cure?"

By now, I was upset. I'd been working with Philip for nearly a year. I thought he understood where I was coming from. Didn't he realize that the majority of doctors in the United States probably thought that the treadmill study was quackery and a waste of time? So many people out there in the medical community believed that SCI was incurable and that there was no point in doing any new research at all. So few doctors were taking the initiative and researching with any sense of urgency. I was so thankful to the team at Kessler for taking on this field of research, which is why I'd expected that someone like Philip would want to at least find out more about a doctor who was breaking new ground.

"I just don't want to advocate anything that could put patients at serious risk," he continued.

I tried to calm down and see it from his perspective. What he was saying was that I was taking a gamble. I knew this. I knew I should probably wait. I had every expectation that Dr. Huang's surgery would be perfected in a couple of years. Maybe research in the United States might even catch up someday, and I could do the surgery without having to travel thousands of miles and spend thousands of dollars. But what was I going to do in the meantime? Sit around watching others get better while I fell behind?

Wait a couple of years? Ten years? Twenty? I was paralyzed right now. Why should I wait? *You* try waiting, Philip!

Then there was my physical therapist, Ken. That same day, after finishing the treadmill session, I was downstairs in the main gym, doing our therapy routine, and I told him all about my trip.

"That's awesome!" he responded. "So when are you going to go? I mean, I know most people will tell you to wait, but if it were me, I would be on the first plane to China."

Finally, I thought, someone who gets it.

Another factor that helped to galvanize my resolve was a PBS documentary about stem-cell research called *The Miracle Cell*. The program didn't mention Dr. Huang, but it did feature a doctor named Carlos Lima who was conducting experimental stem-cell surgery in Lisbon, Portugal. In the Portuguese procedure, doctors harvest cells from the patient's own nose, the theory being that the olfactory nerve cells found in the nose are among the only nerves in the body that regenerate on their own. When these cells are transplanted into a damaged spine, the hope is that they can retain their regenerative properties and induce recovery. Some of Dr. Lima's American spinal-cord-injury patients who had already undergone the surgery were shown in the film. One of these was a nineteen-year-old named Laura Dominguez, who had broken her neck in a car accident in 2001. After she returned from surgery in Portugal, Dr. Stephen Hinderer, medical director of the Rehabilitation Institute of Michigan, was supervising her recovery in Detroit—this was the same institute that Bob Smith, one of Dr. Huang's patients I had read about, had attended after his trip to China. Dr. Hinderer ascertained that while Laura couldn't feel anything below her collarbone before her treatment, since her surgery, she had a degree of sensation as low as her belly button.

Dr. Hinderer spoke of the "incredible potential" of this kind of surgery: "The difference is, I will be able to just say to somebody with a spinal-cord injury, yes, you will walk again, as opposed to telling them life is good from a wheelchair."

I was incredibly excited and energized by the program and Dr. Hinderer's words. I felt motivated. I felt vindicated! I made everyone I knew watch the program, and I watched it over and over again until I had memorized every word. If anyone tried to dissuade me from undergoing surgery, I would say, "Watch *The Miracle Cell!*"

In the coming months, it often felt like China and the surgery had become my main point of discussion. If we had people over for dinner, the subject would inevitably shift to my surgery and all the many issues surrounding this kind of treatment.

"The thing that I find the most outrageous," my dad said, "is that Francesco can't have his surgery right here in the United States. You have to ask yourself why we have fallen so far behind."

"It doesn't help that we have a president who honestly believes he is doing the right thing by virtually banning stem-cell research," my mom chimed in. "Doesn't he know that people desperately need this research to move forward?"

I should point out that my parents are Catholics. They go to church each week. They observe all the religious holidays. My dad says grace at dinner. They live a life of service. They are religious in the truest sense of the word. And they have always been pro–stem-cell research.

"There has to be separation between the state, the Church, and science," my mom insisted.

But we were a long, long way from that ideal. When President Bush announced his embryonic stem cell ruling in 2001, he declared it immoral to use human life for the benefit of another life.

The president argued that he was *protecting* human life because embryos have to be destroyed in order to create the stem-cell lines. Pope John Paul II weighed in and declared the medical use of cells from embryos a grave sin. What Bush and the pope would fail to mention was that these embryos came from fertility clinics and would be destroyed anyway. So why shouldn't those same embryos be used to benefit science, rather than being thrown away? It didn't make any sense. Something more political was going on, at least in the case of the president. Bush was "playing to his base," those people who had helped him get elected in one of the narrowest elections in U.S. history the year before. I just didn't understand how this issue had become so controversial. Didn't these people understand that stem-cell treatments could potentially alleviate so much suffering? That they could potentially hold extraordinary healing powers that could help everything from brain function to heart function? Surely it was in all our best interests to want to support this kind of research.

As fast as I was educating myself, I was also realizing that I had to educate those around me. Most people were supportive, but one particularly devout friend of the family was vocal in his disapproval of our decision.

When I told him that I was all set to go to China, he was quiet for a moment, and then said, "So this is about stem cells?"

"Yes, it's about stem cells. But it's also about getting better. Dr. Huang is reporting some pretty impressive results."

"I have to tell you that I don't agree with this, Francesco," he said gravely.

"But these cells were never going to become humans!" I argued.

"Francesco, I only know that this is wrong and it involves killing life!"

"But how is this different from using a heart from someone who's died for a heart transplant?" I asked him. "Would you say that a heart transplant was killing a person to help a person?"

"Francesco, I don't know so much about this as you. I just know it's wrong."

Since my injury, I had only encountered a small handful of people who were against embryonic stem-cell research and they seemed unshakable in their beliefs. What I was discovering was that they didn't tend to be very educated about the subject. When I asked them about the difference between an embryonic stem cell and an adult stem cell, or the difference between therapeutic cloning and human cloning, they couldn't answer me. I realized that they were confusing stem cells with cloning. They heard the word "stem cells" and immediately began imagining deranged doctors trying to play God. Therapeutic cloning cannot create a human being, because what is being created is a set of cells necessary to the individual patient. For example, a severe burn victim would have *skin* cells created.

"This is about helping people in desperate need," I told our friend. "It's not about playing God and creating human life."

"I don't know, Francesco," he repeated, "I just know I don't agree with it."

"But even if the president and the Church wanted to oppose embryonic stem-cell therapies, then what about supporting alternative research?" I continued. "How much federal money is being allocated for *adult* stem-cell research, which poses no threat to human life—even by the Church's definition?" These types of cells were harvested from human umbilical cords or bone marrow and were already being used successfully to help treat a range of afflictions. It seemed to me that if you were so vehemently against embryonic stem cells, then why not support adult stem-cell research with increased funding in that area? I didn't care where the cure came from. I just wanted the cure.

As time went on, I began to realize that I could use the nay-sayers to strengthen my determination. I needed to convince people—myself included—that I was making an educated deci-sion. I knew I couldn't allow other people's doubts to become my doubts, because if I lived my life that way, where would I be? The people who opposed my decision actually helped me to stand my ground, and this was good, because I had to educate myself so I could counter every argument that came my way. I became a bet-ter advocate for myself and for this decision I had made to go to China. I would rehearse my arguments over and over again until they were lodged in my brain. After all, I had to memorize every-thing. It wasn't like I could just reach for a pen and jot something down.

18

Touchdown

THE NIGHT BEFORE DEPARTURE DAY I LAY AWAKE IN MY BED, unable to sleep. I looked around our living room—now my bedroom—and the regular pang of guilt ran through me. So many nights before falling asleep, I would beg: *Just make this all go away. Make this bad dream vaporize.* My stomach turned, just thinking of how much money my parents were spending on my surgery, on the trip, on me. How would I repay them? How could I prove to them I was worth all of this trouble and expense and pain? Please, please work, I thought. Make these little cells grow.

Finally, worn out from all the anxiety and questioning, I started to slide into much-needed sleep. I awoke at seven a.m. The sun was up, and I could hear my grandmother in the kitchen. I knew she was making espresso, eggs, and the apple cake that we eat like bread. I knew she would be baking more than usual, partly because she was nervous, but also because she wanted to pack us food for the long flight. My sister was running up and down the stairs, hauling suitcases down to the kitchen from her room.

"I've got all of the passports, Mom. Checco, I've got your iPod. It's charged for the flight."

My father was going through his vitamin concoctions, telling me when to take certain antioxidants, what would help with low blood pressure, and what would help to speed healing after the surgery. How many suitcases were we bringing, nine? It looked like a lot, but it wasn't. Much of what we brought were medical supplies we couldn't buy in Beijing. It honestly felt as if we were now moving to China.

Everyone came to the airport to say good-bye: my dad, my brother, and my grandmother. I knew we were all asking the same question: Was this going to work?

"You're going to be great," my dad told me, reading my mind.

Now I just had to get through the fourteen-hour flight. This was my first time on a plane since the injury, and I was nervous. After a few hassles with the airline attendant—who at first said I couldn't board with my wheelchair—we were finally all seated in the aircraft. Thankfully, the flight on Air China would be direct from New York to Beijing, no stopover or connections. As the plane taxied down the runway, I felt like I was beginning a long wait for a surprise birthday party—I was almost sick with nerves and excitement. During the flight, my mother, who was sitting one row ahead of Charlotte and me, would turn around and mouth: "We're going to China!" and we would mouth back: "Yaaaaay!" and wave our arms. No doubt everyone else on the plane thought we were crazy, but it seemed to go with the territory.

Although I had been worried about the flight, I was fine. I didn't break out in one of my sweats—the indicator that I was in pain from sitting in one position for too long—and this was a pleasant surprise. Even so, by the time our plane touched down in Beijing, I was so desperate to get out of the cabin's confines, I would have bum-rushed the exit door if I could have.

A doctor from the hospital met us at the airport and, with the help of his driver, Charlotte and I managed to cram into the doctor's car, with the wheelchair squashed in the trunk. My mom followed with our bags in a taxi.

Through the car's window, I got my first glimpses of Beijing. It was early evening now, and the sun had set, the lights from the big city illuminating the sky in amber and red. The traffic signs on the road were written in red lights, and it was so strange to see the Chinese characters everywhere. Construction was in full force, in preparation for the Olympics in 2008, still four years away. Everywhere I looked, there was a large crane on top of a half-finished building.

Suddenly, I felt my eyes and nose get congested and I started to sneeze.

"Allergies?" I asked. I'd never had allergies this late in the spring.

I looked at my sister, noticing that her eyes were red and watery too. As we would soon learn, we were suffering from the effects of pollution. Outside the car, the mist over the city that we thought was fog was actually smog. I kept thinking it would clear sooner or later, like a passing storm, but it would stay hanging there for the whole of our visit.

For the rest of the short journey, the doctor told us about the other American and European patients who were at the hospital. "Your surgery is scheduled for next week," he announced.

Whoa, next week. That was really soon. All of this time and build-up, and all of a sudden it was next week. I felt a wrench of nervous anticipation.

The hospital was in the heart of the city, and before long, we pulled up to a large complex of buildings. Twenty hours after leaving home in Bronxville, we had finally reached our destination. The hospital building itself was huge, and the way it was laid out made it look even bigger. It was shaped like a U, with its two sides jutting toward us. Everything was gray and concrete. There must have been one hundred cars parked like sardines in the center courtyard, in front of the immense entrance. We managed the transfer into my wheelchair, went up the ramp, and entered the front doors of the international patients' wing.

The wing itself was compact—no longer than fifty meters—and contained five patient rooms. Everything was a wash of white, and the marble floors from the entrance extended to the wing. The patient rooms were on the left, with a large reception area behind a low-level glassed-off reception area to the right. It was hot in there, we were tired, and we had a dozen large suitcases to unpack.

"Here are your rooms," our doctor said. "We gave you two, since there are three of you."

They were nice, basic rooms, with two large windows along the far wall. The rooms seemed clean, but the windows were dirty from dust from the construction going on nearby. My mother started to clean the floors with a mop she had already found in the supply closet by the entrance. Before Charlotte could even unpack one suitcase, our mother was pouring bleach into a bucket.

"Is it *that* dirty?" I asked, exhausted.

"Do you want to take that chance?" By now, she had almost finished mopping our floor, and she was right. The water turned black, filled with soot—not the kind of thing you want to see in a hospital room, even on the floor.

Soon after we arrived, one of the nurses walked in to introduce herself. "Hello, my name is Bird. It is so nice to meet you." Her hair was in a sharp bob, and her big smile was very cheerful. "I have a fan. Do you want it?"

"Oh, yes, thank you," said my mother. "It's so hot. We were told there wouldn't be air-conditioning, but a fan would be great."

"Are you hungry?" my mother asked me after Bird left.

"Weirdly, no," I replied. This was strange for me. I'm never *not* hungry. Maybe it was nerves, or maybe it was the heat, coupled with the smog in the air, but I had completely lost my appetite.

The journey had taken everything out of me. Unable to eat dinner, I fell into a restless, exhausted sleep.

We spent the following days getting to know the other nurses and patients on the international ward. My neighbor was also from the United States. She was suffering from advanced ALS, that terrible, debilitative disease. Another ALS patient was from Belgium. There was a man from Ohio who had injured his spinal cord in a construction accident, and two patients from Japan, also with spinal-cord injuries. Everyone came in and out of one another's rooms to say hi. It felt like we were living in a sort of college dorm. People were friendly; there was a lot of camaraderie, a feeling of being in the same boat.

Wherever we went out in Beijing, however, we felt like fish out of water. We came to the conclusion that a wheelchair was an uncommon sight in the city, because little kids would stop in their tracks when I came into view, their mothers pulling at them to make them move; but then when the mothers saw what their children were looking at, they would stare as well.

"Man, it seems like they've never seen a handicapped person before," Charlotte said as she popped a big wheelie to get over what looked like a six-inch curb.

"They're looking at my shiny teeth and good skin, dontcha know," I joked.

One of the other problems we were encountering while getting around the city was crossing the streets. Every time we went out, the first thing we had to do was make it to the other side of a busy six-lane road. Even when the traffic lights were in our favor, this didn't help, because the street was very wide, and some cars turned left or right despite the red lights. When we were two lanes away from getting to the other side, the lights turned green, at which point the cars charged forward like angry bulls, their engines roaring.

"Don't worry. They'll slow down. They have to see us," my mother said.

But . . . was it just me, or were they speeding up? Did we do something to annoy them? Now they were definitely speeding up!

"Oh my God. Stop!" My sister was running, pushing me, waving her arms, screaming at the drivers. My mother started waving at the cars too. The whole time I was holding on to my armrests for support, so I didn't fall over.

Top speed for my wheelchair is a brisk walk, or maybe an impish jog—nothing Olympian in the least. I'm guessing potato-sack-race speed is a good rule of measure for me. Any faster, and the front wheels start shaking and the whole frame vibrates. Yet here we were, all of these cars coming toward a man in a wheelchair with two women pushing him, all three of us screaming at the top of our lungs, and none of the drivers slowing down. It seemed like every time we crossed the street in Beijing, we were rolling the dice. It got to the point where Charlotte put on her running shoes to push me. As we got ready to embark on a large intersection, I made the sign of the cross, and we would scream—"*Goooooo!*" We started to plan our excursions based upon how few street crossings there were.

"They're such nice people when they're not driving," my mom pointed out. "They help us whenever we're having a tough time with grocery bags or getting into a building. Then they get into their cars, and it looks like they want to run us over!"

Then one afternoon, Dr. Huang came to see me in my room. He was with two other of his surgeons and three nurses, all talking quietly.

"Hi, Mr. Clark," he said. "Your surgery will be in three days."

It honestly felt like my high-school principal had just popped into the room and cheerfully shouted, "Surprise! Final exam tomorrow!" I was so taken aback, I almost lost the small amount of lunch I'd been able to eat.

"We will begin EMG testing tomorrow morning, blood tests, your MRI scans, and pulmonary exams. Please sleep well so you will be ready."

"Dr. Huang," I wanted to know, "what will the surgery be like?"

"We will turn you onto your stomach so that we can inject cells above and below your injury," he explained. "You will need to rest for quite some time afterwards." As I was discovering, Dr. Huang was a man of few words.

He picked up my right arm, feeling it and turning it over. With his other hand he opened and closed his fist in front of me.

"Oh, I can't do that yet," I explained. "My arms are very weak. I hope they will get stronger with the surgery."

He patted my back and smiled at me. "You will get better," he said.

FINALLY, THE BIG DAY DAWNED. I woke up two hours before the surgery prep time. People were milling about outside my room—the nurses, some doctors, and some of the other patients who had come to wish me good luck.

I entered the operating room. Seeing the surgery table made my head spin. So much anticipation building up to this moment.

Two nurses were prepping the room. One of them had opened a supply closet and was taking out IV bags and other tools needed for the next couple of hours. She dropped something. It sounded like an IV bag. She picked it up, sighed, and then she dropped it again. I certainly didn't find it comforting to see someone prepping the room like this. I could imagine her saying, "I am such a klutz! Keep it together. Where did I put my glasses?"

"You're not going to do that during my surgery," I half-joked. "I'm not going to wake up with Junior Mints in my brain, right?" At home, I was used to joking with my doctors, therapists, and nurses. It helped me to relax and lightened the atmosphere. But here I was dealing with the language barrier. The nurse definitely didn't get the joke, but I think she got the gist of my concern.

I waited. I was now on the operating table, and I was becoming uncomfortable. All of a sudden, both nurses were focused on me. One was preparing a clear mask while the other was talking: "Breathe this. Deep breath."

She was holding the mask with her left hand and leaning in close to my face.

My mind went gray. My last memory before closing my eyes was seeing the bright lights glaring above my head.

19

Post-Op

I WOKE UP AS WE WERE REENTERING MY ROOM. THERE WERE
five or six nurses and aides on either side of me, pushing the cot
and steering it, everyone talking. Several of the other patients
had come out of their rooms. I could hear their voices but didn't
have the strength to say anything yet. I opened my eyes halfway—
just for long enough to confirm that the operation was over and
that I was alive—then I slipped back into sleep. The next time I
awoke, it felt like ten minutes later. In fact, I'd been asleep for
hours.

I opened my eyes fully. Suddenly, I realized that there was a
TV camera crew in my room. They came toward me, half a dozen
strangers thrusting cameras and microphones in my direction,
talking loudly in broken English with heavy Chinese accents. I'd
just come out of major surgery. All I could do was close my eyes
and hope for them to go away.

"Mom—he's awake!" Charlotte called to my mom, who was on
the phone in the hallway.

I opened my eyes again and smiled back at my sister.

I told her, "Take photos. I want to see what this all looks like."

"Really? You don't want to just—"

"No. Take photos."

As I spoke, I realized I felt something.

"I feel something," I told Charlotte.

"What?"

"I can feel my ribs!"

"No way. Yay!"

I grinned from ear to ear. Charlotte snapped the photo.

My mom walked in, and Charlotte told her the news. They both started to laugh and cheer. They had waited eight hours for the surgery to be over and for me to wake up. Yes, I was covered in tubes and wiped out by morphine, but even so, they could tell I was OK. In fact, I was more than OK.

"I can feel most of my arms," I told them. "Not just the insides of them anymore. The entire arm!" My right triceps actually felt achy.

"Really?"

"Yes, really. But this tube coming out of my neck is incredibly annoying."

There were two glass IV bottles to my left, dangling from a metal stand. Multiple tubes went into my body, one into a series of tubes that had been implanted around my collarbone, like a port. It felt like I had a giant wire lodged inside my body. I could feel its loop going around my collarbone, and all I wanted to do was rip it out. Another IV bottle was hooked up to my foot, which was something else I'd never seen before.

Charlotte and my mother explained that I wouldn't need the port for too long. They also told me that Dr. Huang had found more damage to my spinal cord than expected.

"He had to use more cells on you than he normally does," Charlotte told me.

My mother went to call my dad to tell him the news. Not

only had I gotten through the operation, I was feeling results already.

I closed my eyes and fell back into a deep, deep sleep.

When I woke up again Bird, the nurse, was at my bedside. The port going into the top of my chest had six or seven stubby ends that enabled her to inject my medication, but as she moved the wires, they felt as if they were pulling at my insides. To make matters worse, I was constantly aware of the three-inch-long incision and stitches in the back of my neck. There was pressure there; not in my throat, but where the skin had been parted in surgery. I could sense that either side wasn't fully connected to itself—an extremely disquietening feeling.

Even so, it was hard to be calm and stay in bed. I was excited. I wanted to talk to people. I could feel parts of my body I hadn't felt since my accident. The areas where I had regained sensation were hypersensitive, especially my ribs. I found myself constantly rubbing them with the underside of my arms, because even the slightest ruffle in the air when I moved my arms was like a giant breeze. My sensitivity was so extreme that it felt as if I was naked even when I was dressed. Every time I rubbed my ribs, I thought: *Incredible.*

Dr. Huang came that evening to check up on my progress.

I told him right away about the new sensation in my ribs and my arms.

"Very good," he said calmly. "Every patient is so different." One girl could feel her toes immediately. There were others who could feel their bladders. Some people felt pain. Some started to sweat.

Dr. Huang gave me my prognosis: "Everything looks fine," he informed me. "But you have to always remember that surgery is not the answer on its own. As soon as you're strong enough, you have to start intensive physical therapy again."

Of course, I understood that I had to continue with therapy, but even so, I wanted to know if there was anything else he could do for me.

"Can I come back and have a second operation? Is it possible I could get more feeling back?" I asked.

"We can do a second operation, yes, but only if you stop making progress," he told me. "If you continue to recover and gain more muscle movement, then no, I won't operate on you again."

"So what can I expect to feel in three, five months' time? In a year?" If I could feel my ribs and my arms, then what were the possibilities for the future?

"I can't tell you that," said Dr. Huang, shaking his head. "Everyone is different. What I can tell you is that you have to keep doing physical therapy. Keep working at it."

I got it. Dr. Huang was reluctant to set specific expectations with something that was an experimental procedure. Even so, I hadn't expected to feel my ribs or arms, so as far as I was concerned, anything was possible. In the coming days, I became aware of sensation in my spine, right at the site of my injury. This would be something I'd need to get used to. From now on, I would have a constant tickling, buzzing feeling in my spine.

While so much progress was exciting, I was exhausted. I felt as if I had just run five marathons. The surgery affected my entire nervous system and brain. My blood pressure was way below normal, and I was still getting morphine to deal with the pain. I stayed in bed for five days, drifting in and out of sleep. After five days, I could sit in a chair for about an hour before going right back to bed. Even sitting up was a challenge—I was having to acclimate my body to being upright again. After six days, it was time to leave my hospital bed so that another patient could be accommodated. We had to move to a nearby hotel. My mother stayed to help get me settled, but immediately afterward she flew back home to return to work. Charlotte stayed with me until I was well enough to travel.

My lack of appetite was still an issue. Even eating the smallest mouthful of food was a huge effort. While I was picking at breakfast I thought to myself, "Ugh, I have to have lunch in three hours." When my sister ordered sushi for lunch, I said to her, "Just tell me how many pieces I have to eat." I couldn't face even the smallest bite, and ordinarily I love sushi. In fact, ordinarily I love anything edible. Dinner came around, and instead of looking forward to food, I dreaded having to force-feed myself.

My sister couldn't believe it.

"Do I know you?" she asked. "Did they do a personality transplant while you were in the operating room?"

Charlotte and I were alone in China for about two and a half weeks, during which time I lost twenty-five pounds. By the end of my trip, I couldn't wait to go home. Every second of the flight back to New York, I anticipated landing. The whole family came to meet us at JFK, a real welcoming committee. The Clark family team picked up where it left off: Mom giving the orders, Dad getting the suitcases, my brother going to open the van, all of us packed inside two cars alongside the mountains of luggage.

When I got home, it was obvious that my grandmother had been cooking for days. There was the usual clamor around the kitchen table. That night, I devoured platefuls of fresh homemade pasta. There was gnocchi fritti, one of my favorite dishes, multiple courses, pastries for dessert. I ate and ate and ate. The relief I felt being home was enormous. Collectively, my family had put on a brave face in the run-up to the surgery, but all the planning, anticipation, and anxiety had been hard on them too. It had taken a toll on everyone. We were all happy; we were all ravenous, and suddenly we were all exhausted.

20

Detroit

AS I EMERGED FROM THE RECOVERY PERIOD, I BEGAN RE-structuring my therapy. My new areas of sensation actually set me back for a time. It's hard to use muscles that you haven't used in three years. I couldn't work these areas of feeling with anything resembling delicacy or subtlety. The muscles around my ribs and in my arms would either clench or not work at all. I began the slow work of relearning a range of movement. Once again, my days were filled with physical therapy, but in the beginning, I had to take things slowly. I didn't regain my full strength for another three months after my return from China. It was frustrating, but I knew it had been worth it. I was able to feel my ribs, move my arms, sense the buzzing in my spine. There was no way I would go back to that dead, dull, nothingness of before. I might be tired, I might be confused, but I felt alive.

Now that China was over, I knew that I wanted to push things to the next level, and as far as I was concerned, this meant getting myself to Detroit. This was where a doctor of rehabilitative medicine named Steven Hinderer was working on a physical-therapy program that was the most progressive of its kind. I'd first learned about Dr. Hinderer in the TV program I had watched called *The Miracle Cell* about stem-cell therapies that had featured the work of Dr. Lima in Portugal. Many of Dr. Lima's patients—as well as Dr. Huang's patients—would then visit Detroit to work on their rehabilitation. Dr. Hinderer was doing nontraditional physical therapy with people who had undergone these surgeries. My parents agreed with me: The next step was Detroit. As Charlotte was starting medical school, my mom agreed to come with me.

FROM THE BEGINNING, it was clear that Detroit was going to be a productive experience. Dr. Hinderer's clinic was a completely different environment from any other rehabilitative setting I had encountered. People had come from all over—from Seattle, New York, Idaho, California, and Canada. They didn't have to be there: they wanted to be there. The therapists wanted to be there too—Dr. Hinderer had created a positive and stimulating place where everyone could contribute and bring new knowledge to the table. I was excited about spending my days around people who had undergone experimental surgeries. I was eager to spend time with these therapists who were obviously so enthusiastic about working with patients. I wanted to learn and improve, and I felt that this was what Detroit was going to give me. It was the kind of innovative approach I could have only dreamed of when I first began my adventures in physical therapy back in New York.

Although a lot of the other patients had thoracic injuries— meaning they could already use their fingers, abs, and backs normally—there were two other patients with spinal-cord injuries at similar levels to mine. In a typical rehabilitative hospital setting you spend a lot of time talking about insurance and how insurance will pay for your therapy. But in Detroit, the first question anyone asked was: "What do you want to do to get better?"

The question alone was empowering. It was proactive, and it put the emphasis on the patient's wellbeing rather than the extent of his or her coverage. At the same time, the therapists were asking for a lot of input from the patients, and this felt good. Instead of taking us through a set of predetermined exercises, *we* were being asked to come up with activities that *we* wanted to do. Then we would figure out how to do them in collaboration with our therapists.

I decided that I wanted to learn how to balance on one of those big physio balls, the kind that look like overgrown beach balls. The first time I tried it, I felt as if I was dangling off the edge of a cliff even with a therapist supporting me. It was terrifying.

John, my therapist, was a man of few words, but he always got to the point.

"What? It's fine," he said with a shrug. "It's just a ball. Figure out what you can do next."

I'd never been challenged in this way before. John didn't want me to be passive and just do as I was told. He wanted me to be inventive and to overcome my fears. Before long, I could sit on the ball—with John's help—without feeling like I was about to fall flat on my face. Next I wanted to try rolling, so we worked on that. I had the idea to try crawling, so we worked on how to do that. Everything about the Detroit therapy was nontraditional, inventive, aggressive. I was being asked to make imaginative leaps, to push myself in new directions.

It was in Detroit that I first began to work on kicking.

In one of my earliest sessions, John put me on a massage table. He started moving my limbs, exploring my range of motion. All of a sudden, I could feel that I was about to have an involuntary spasm in my leg. This sometimes happened during therapy. The muscles would cramp up and then my leg would jerk. I'd always been taught that a spasm is a bad thing. Whenever this had happened in the past, the therapist would start massaging my leg to calm things down so that the spasm would go away.

On the table with John, I could feel that the muscles were tightening in my leg, so I said to him, "I'm sorry. Just wait a minute and the spasm will stop."

"OK, so what did that feel like?" John asked.

"I could feel a slight tightening in the muscles before the spasm," I told him.

"Can you connect with that and do it again?" he asked me.

"Sure. I mean, I can try."

I tried it, and sure enough, the more I focused on the feeling of the spasm, the stronger it got. Something amazing was happening. John was helping me to reconnect with feeling in my legs. Until now, my legs had been sandbags. The idea of moving my legs had become so foreign to me it felt as pointless as looking at a piece of paper across the room and thinking, "OK, move that with your eyes." But what John was encouraging me to do was to re-learn the first step in voluntary movement—he was helping me to connect intention and feeling. In theory, since my accident, I had lost this connection completely. But if I could *feel* a spasm in my leg, and *think* about working with that feeling, then over time maybe I would get to a point where I could command the spasm so that it would become voluntary movement, initiated by me and by the power of my thought.

I already had a general idea of how to stimulate a spasm. I knew that sometimes if I tensed my whole body, it would cause my leg to jerk. Now, instead of resting and calming the spasm when I felt a tightening in my legs, I would try to keep the feeling going. I would do this by thinking and by tensing my body. At first, my leg kicks were jerky and not smooth at all. My leg would shake crazily. But as time went on, I could feel the muscles getting really tight—stronger than I'd ever felt before. Then, as I started to try to control the movement with my thought, I would realize that I could make the spasms stop or I could make them start again. Every day in Detroit—and every day since then—I've been working on that control.

I couldn't wait to show my kicks to my mom.

"Hey, Francesco!" she cheered. "C'mon. More, more, more!"

It felt so good to share my progress with her. This was confirmation for both of us that the trip had been worth it. We felt as if we were getting something done. When I spoke with the other patients with spinal-cord injuries who had also been taught to work with spasms, we all agreed that this new way of thinking was nothing short of mind-blowing.

Suddenly a whole universe of thought-feeling connection was opening up to me. I was realizing how much I still had to learn. It wasn't just my usual therapy routine anymore. I was working on increasing my muscle control in my legs by *thinking*. With more control came more deliberate movements. The leg kicks became smoother, slower. My legs no longer felt like dead wood attached to my body. I was a long way from walking, but I knew I was breaking new ground.

I was learning and making progress—and getting to spend time with other patients who had undergone the surgeries—but even so, there were many aspects of the Detroit experience that were tough on me and my mom. I felt guilty about taking her away from home for so long. I worried that it was too much for her, and that my dad was struggling to keep everything going at home. We had picked the worst time of year to make the trip. It was winter, and it was freezing. It snowed every day while we were there, thick white snow under uninterrupted gray clouds. Luckily, we didn't have to go too far to get to therapy, because the wind chill was insane: Just stepping outside meant confronting a freezing gale. We were living in a basic, rather drab dormitory apartment adjacent to the clinic. We ate there, slept there, watched TV there. The whole day was about therapy and nothing else. This went on and on for three months.

Part of the problem was that I just wasn't used to having so much time on my hands. In Detroit, my commute to the therapy sessions took exactly three minutes, unlike my usual two-hour drive to New Jersey and back. In Detroit, when I wasn't doing therapy, my other waking hours were free. I had become so used to racing to Kessler each day that I'd forgotten what it was like to have more than a minute to e-mail friends or read a book or just stare out the window. One day in Detroit, out of sheer boredom— and because I literally had nothing else to do—I switched on my laptop and started writing. Since returning from China I had more mobility and muscle strength in my arms and hands, which meant that it was easier for me to type. I began writing funny little stories about my childhood. I wasn't thinking of showing them to anyone; I just needed something to keep myself entertained that didn't involve watching reruns on TV.

In Detroit, I retreated into the bubble of my childhood memories, a period of my life so far removed from where I was in the present moment. I wrote about the trips to Italy that we would take in the summertime; my dad and his endless attempts to turn us into perfect little Catholics; my mom and her dry sense of humor with us as children. My childhood had been a very happy one—we were an extremely active family, always learning, on the go. I would show these vignettes to my mom, who would laugh at them and tell me to send them on to my sister, brother, and dad. Then I started writing about Detroit and all the crazy therapy that I was doing. I started describing China and everything that happened there. Often I wrote long e-mails to friends where I would just vent. Detroit created a void where I was forced to become more creative. It was around this time that I began working on some of the writings that ended up becoming this book. I was beginning to connect the different parts of my life, seeing my story as more of a whole, rather than the "before" and "after" of my accident.

As I wrote and reflected, it became increasingly obvious that when I returned home, I didn't want to go back to my regimen of driving to New Jersey each day. Without all those hours spent in the van, I'd actually have some time to continue thinking, writing, and exploring other interests. The patients I was meeting in Detroit were all doing things with their lives *besides* therapy. One of them was an advocate for people with disabilities. One of them had his own real-estate company. One woman had actually started the rehab department where we were doing our therapy. It was truly inspiring to be around people who were overcoming the limits imposed on them by their disabilities and forging ahead. Everyone I was meeting in Detroit had moved beyond the trauma of their initial injuries to find ways to help themselves, and others, too.

"There's no way I can go back to that routine," I told my mom. "I'm sick of spending all my time in the van."

My mom completely agreed. She immediately suggested converting our garage into a makeshift gym so that I would have enough space for all the necessary equipment at home.

"And if I never have to make that drive to New Jersey again, I won't complain," she said.

"OK," I told my mom, "let's do it. But on one condition: I do not want you and Dad to pay for all of this."

I had other ideas. It seemed as if everyone I met in Detroit had been having regular fund-raisers to raise money for their therapy. Why didn't I do the same? My mother and I began making plans. I wrote to friends and told them I wanted to have a fund-raiser. We began putting the word out to local gyms and at my dad's office to find independent trainers and therapists to work with me at home. We needed to find people who would feel comfortable about continuing the therapy that I'd been learning in Detroit. I wanted to be around trainers and therapists who would empower me to be inventive and proactive. I was excited to go back to Bronxville—not only because I was going to see my family and friends for the first time in many months, but because we were going to change our whole approach to my day-to-day therapy. We were taking matters into our own hands.

Psychologically, I was shifting from being the person dealing with the aftermath of a traumatic event to becoming someone who wanted to live. I was tired of always being a patient, and being patient while waiting for a cure. I wanted to do something to become part of the cure and part of a bigger voice. I had so much energy but no outlet, and the thought of doing only physical therapy for six hours a day, every day, made me feel worthless. I had been so fixated on finding the next step in my recovery that it had become the *only* thing I did. The China surgery and getting to Detroit had been my focus—my obsession—for so many months. It was like I was about to graduate, and like all graduates, I had to figure out what to do with myself now.

I was twenty-seven years old. This was a time when I was seeing all my friends from college getting promoted, going to graduate school, getting married. Meanwhile, I was at a standstill. All I did was therapy. I knew how important it was to my recovery, but at the same time, it left me only a half an hour a day to read or write an e-mail or pursue any kind of independent interest. After Detroit, some part of me was seeking a new path, but I had no idea where to look for it or what it would look like once I saw it.

I knew I wanted to find something that was mine. I wanted to work again. I wanted to earn money, use my brain, and be creative. I wanted to get back to being more like me.

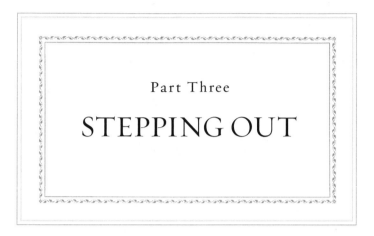

Part Three

STEPPING OUT

21

~~~

What Now?

WHILE I'D BEEN AWAY IN CHINA AND DETROIT, MY PARENTS
had made some changes around the house. I was no longer sleeping in the living room. My whole setup had been moved to the
sunroom—a square room on the side of the house that served as
our TV room. These were my new quarters. There was my bed,
my desk, my computer, my bureau, all my stuff. Evidently my
mother had enough of me taking over the whole of her living
room, but more important, she was recognizing that I needed
my own space, set apart from the family, where I could have some
privacy. From the moment I saw my new room, I loved it. It was a
place I associated with relaxing and having fun, and with sunshine. Tall, narrow windows on three sides filled my bedroom
with light throughout the day.

When I woke up, my eyes were at window-level, looking out
onto the leaves on the bushes, birds in the clusters of branches.
Early morning sun danced on my face. I didn't feel as if I was
inside: I felt as if I was outside. The move to the sunroom was a
breath of fresh air. I began spending all my spare time in the sunroom, sitting at my desk, looking out over the wishing well on the

back patio, watching the sky, the trees, the flowers, just thinking. My mom had put some of her mineral rocks out on the patio, yellow and purple quartz. The sun bouncing off them created fantastic flashes of soothing violets and ambers. My room was a perfect cube shape, but with all these views. I began to think of the sunroom as a visual depiction of my life. My injury had boxed me in, given me all these boundaries with seemingly immovable edges. But China and Detroit had been a window. By using my imagination and looking out of the box, I had been able to see my way forward.

Now that I was back from Detroit, my problem was that I had to find my way forward all over again.

Since my accident, I'd been living with a growing sense of urgency. At the moment I was injured, I came close to death. In that split second before I was rescued, I felt my life slipping away from me. It's a very strange thing to know that you only just made it. For the first few years after my accident, I had no idea how to deal with this newfound awareness that life could be taken from you in an instant. Three years later, I knew I no longer wanted to spend my whole life in therapy. I wanted to do something more meaningful. I wanted to make the most of all the potential I believed that my life could offer me while I still could.

This feeling of "no time to lose" was compounded by the sad news about Christopher Reeve that we all received in October of the previous year, just before I left for Detroit. I had been in the van en route to New Jersey, going to Kessler when I heard. Usually, I was always so excited to hear anything about my hero. If he made the smallest amount of progress or started championing some innovative trial, I wanted to know everything about it. Just the knowledge of his existence and all the work he did on behalf of everyone with SCI gave me hope. And so at first, I couldn't believe it was true. Superman couldn't have died. He was what? Fifty-one, fifty-two years old? Way too young. This was someone who always defied the odds. Immediately after his accident, he'd stopped breathing for something like three minutes, and even so, he'd survived. He'd had serious health problems before, and despite this, he'd continued to make progress with his recovery—more than anyone had thought possible.

But there it was: the newscaster announcing again that Superman had died from cardiac arrest. At that moment, I just wanted to go to bed. I wanted to go to sleep and pretend this never happened, as if closing my eyes would erase it all magically. I'd heard the words, but I couldn't believe them. I decided I needed to get to Kessler because everyone there would know exactly what had happened. They were going to tell me that he hadn't died, that he had contracted pneumonia and was now getting better. Something, *anything*.

No such good news awaited me when I arrived. One look at Nicole, my occupational therapist—usually so sunny—confirmed my worst fears.

When I asked her if it was true, she nodded sadly. "His heart failed."

All I wanted to do was go home. I didn't know what else to do. I wanted everything to just stop so we could acknowledge what was taking place. I didn't want to be sitting there doing finger exercises. The guy to my right had SCI. My other neighbor had had a stroke. Nobody knew what to say.

Finally someone muttered, "It's just so sad." I knew we were all thinking the same thing: If Superman couldn't do it, how can I?

As soon as I got back home that evening, I switched on the TV and the computer. I needed to know everything. I went online, but nothing could be updated fast enough for me. I was glued to the

news. I needed to hear every single word that was said about him. I
had to know more. I needed to absorb every detail because, on
some level, I still couldn't believe it was true.

I kept asking "How?" I was looking for reasons. How did this
happen? What could have been done? Why hadn't things turned
out differently?

He had been doing so much for people with disabilities, and
now he was gone. Who else could do what he had done? There
wasn't anyone who could bring this kind of attention to the need
for a cure. The whole time I'd been injured, I'd had a feeling that
someone had my back. What were we all going to do now?

I couldn't stop thinking about what had happened. I just
wanted to focus on it and put everything else on pause. I didn't
want to go to physical therapy. I didn't want to go through my
usual routine. I had read every obituary, and every word just made
me more and more aware of what we had lost. This was someone
who had started a foundation, traveled the world and met with
research scientists, testified in Congress, gave weekly speeches,
and did countless interviews about the importance of research
into a cure. Despite all his limitations, his life since his injury had
been full, active, meaningful. If I could achieve one iota of what
he had achieved with his life, then I would have been happy, but I
was a long way from doing that.

I knew it was time to start asking myself "How can I help?"
Finding an answer to this question became my obsession. It would
keep me up at night. It consumed me. What could I do? I wanted
to put my energy into something that would actively benefit the
SCI community. But I wasn't some big-shot celebrity—quite the
opposite. My days were spent in physical therapy. I wasn't involved with any causes or committees. I didn't know senators or
groundbreaking researchers or millionaires. So what was I going
to do?

After I got back from Detroit, I tried to come up with ideas
for how to expand my horizons.

"You should play wheelchair basketball," people would say.
Someone thought I should go skydiving. Someone else had the
bright idea of wheelchair rugby: "They knock themselves out of
their chairs!"

To which I could only reply, "Um, no thank you."

These weren't the sports that I did before my injury—and although I think it's great that others do them, they just weren't
for me. I wanted to find something I felt passionate about, something that I loved, so that I had a chance to excel at it and some
way of contributing.

Someone suggested that I should try to go back to my old job
at *Harper's Bazaar*. I would have loved that, but it was simply out of
the question. Being an editorial assistant at a fashion magazine
involved literally running around on your feet all day. There would
be no way I could keep up with the pace.

Then I got a phone call.

"Francesco? Hi, this is Mary. We're starting an advisory committee for people with disabilities, and we were wondering if
you'd be interested in joining."

I'd never met Mary, although she lived just a couple of houses
away from us. She'd heard about me through friends in the area.
On the phone that day, she told me about her young son, who has
Down syndrome, and how she wanted to advocate for better facilities for the disabled, especially in local schools and summer
camps. She knew that I was in a very different situation from her
son, and that was why she wanted me on board, so she could get
my perspective on things. Even over the phone, I could sense her
energy and enthusiasm.

"We're meeting in one week to talk about this with two local
officials," she told me. "If you'd like to join us, it would be great."

I had to say yes. What else was I doing? Why shouldn't I? The meeting was scheduled to take place in the Bronxville Library the following week.

I put down the phone. I had just agreed to attend an actual meeting. I hadn't done something like this in a very long time. Immediately, I looked down at my bright blue paper hospital pants, the same kind that I had been wearing every day since my accident. To complete my outfit, I had a white T-shirt with a faded American flag on it, the same one that I had worn pretty much without interruption for three years—except for weekends when I changed into a long-sleeved cotton shirt that was fraying along the sleeves and collar. Every few weeks, my mom would suggest that I get some new clothes, but I always told her no. I didn't want to. I didn't care about my appearance anymore. The paper pants and T-shirt—along with my shaved head so that I didn't have to comb my hair—this was my uniform. I dressed this way so I wouldn't draw attention to myself. I hated the idea of people feeling sorry for me, so I thought the best way to avoid this was to blend into the background altogether. If someone had given me a cloak of invisibility, I would have worn it, but until then, I was sticking with my paper pants.

Needless to say, this wasn't the way I was raised. In our family, you'd never wear sneakers if you were going to a meeting. You didn't wear shorts and T-shirts, either. My mother and grandmother would consider that a very "non-Italian" way of dressing. I had been brought up to take a certain level of care in how I presented myself, whether that was reflected in what I was wearing or how I contributed to the conversation. And now I was actually contemplating going to a meeting in town with a group of people I'd never met before, in my paper pants and worn-out T-shirt.

My mother walked into my room.

"Mom, I want to stop wearing these stupid pants," I told her.

"Does that mean I can throw them all out?" she asked.

"Yes, you can!"

"If I never see another pair of paper pants, I will be so happy. What about these?" She was holding up the long-sleeved shirt I wore all the time.

"Garbage! Ugly."

"Yay! Finally." My mother was smiling ear to ear. "So, that conversation must have gone well. What did Mary say?"

"That they're starting an advisory committee and that she wants me to join. We're meeting in one week."

THE AFTERNOON OF THE MEETING, I put on a pair of workout pants and an actual new shirt with a collar. Not exactly Prada, but good enough. I was ready to find out exactly what I could do to help.

There were six of us meeting that day. Besides Mary and me, there was a teacher who worked in the next town over, two Bronxville town officials, and another person with a spinal-cord injury whose name was Julie, also from Bronxville. Now that I was faced with the prospect of speaking in front of so many strangers, I felt genuinely nervous. This had never been a problem for me before my injury. In my old life, I would rarely feel timid in social or professional situations. But it had been so long since I'd been out in the world, I had forgotten how to do this. The minute the meeting began, everyone immediately began talking while I remained silent.

Mary wanted to establish the goals of the committee, what we were going to work on, and how we were going to achieve this. She wanted to talk about her son and his specific needs, but also the needs of older people in the community, many of whom were shut-ins because it was so hard to get around. Bronxville is an old town, with many steps and very few ramps. Even the local park had five steps at the main entrance. If you had a cane or you were in a chair, the park was basically off limits, which makes no sense because older people are the ones who can make the best use of the park during the week.

Then Julie started talking about the Americans with Disabilities Act.

"It's the law," she pointed out. "If you have a public space, it has to be accessible. So why doesn't the park have a ramp?"

I had no idea about the Americans with Disabilities Act. I knew that a lot of places had become completely inaccessible to me since my accident, but I'd gotten to the point where I didn't think to question why or if anything could be done. One of the reasons I visited the library as much as I did was that there was a ramp, and there was parking. But even the library lacked the information I sorely needed.

"What about starting some kind of information center for the disabled?" I suggested. "Right here at the library? Somewhere you could go to pick up pamphlets and get advice on your rights, or getting parking permits."

Everyone seemed to think this was a good idea, and so it became one of our goals.

Now I was on a roll. I was actually in a room full of people, having a conversation about something that mattered to me. I was using my brain to help solve problems. People were asking for my opinion, and I was discovering that I had a point of view.

I left the meeting on a high, feeling like I was going to change the universe—or at least the small universe of Bronxville. Over dinner that night, I told my parents about everything that had happened.

"One of the first things we want to do is to get a ramp put in the Section-8 housing," I jabbered to Mom and Dad. "Can you believe? There's a handicapped child living there, and he can't even leave his apartment, because there isn't a ramp. And it's the law—there has to be a ramp. So I can't imagine that it will take too long to get that done. . . ."

I had a lot to learn. Something as simple as putting in a concrete ramp at the local park would take two and a half years of meetings, phone calls, and planning before it was finally installed. We had to cut through a mountain of red tape before the town could get funding. Then the architectural drawings had to be drafted, revised, and approved before the work could even begin. I was learning that when you're dealing with local officialdom, nothing happens in a hurry. But along with Mary and the other participants, I felt committed to our goals. We continued to meet to ensure that local developments and activities included *all* citizens. We spoke out about handicapped parking spots, accessibility to stores, sidewalk cutouts, and state and local support programs. We campaigned and eventually succeeded in having that ramp put in the local housing complex so that the disabled child could enter and leave his home.

My mind was yearning for this kind of stimulation. Deciding to join Mary's group had a wholly positive effect on my life. It broke me out of myself. I was no longer spending every minute of the day thinking about "me and my therapy." I knew I wasn't effecting change on a global scale—Christopher Reeve I was not—but I was doing what I could in my own hometown. And I liked that. Suddenly I didn't want to be invisible anymore. I wanted to get noticed, to speak out, and have people hear what I had to say. I had gotten so caught up in my body, and how I was going to mend it, that I had forgotten I also had a brain.

22

Jasmine Absolute

MARY'S PHONE CALL AND THE COMMITTEE MEETINGS HAD the immediate effect of prising me out of my shell. The more time I spent out in the world, the more I *wanted* to be out in the world. I gained confidence from each interaction. I was feeling increasingly comfortable in my skin—and a big part of the reason for this was that I was actually more comfortable *about* my skin.

Around the time I got back from Detroit, my formerly red, flaking, acne-ridden skin had finally started to improve. For three years, my bad skin had become just another reason to shrink from life and to avoid meeting new people. Like the paper pants and my utilitarian haircut, my skin was an excuse for hibernating. "Who wants to spend time with someone who looks like this?" I reasoned. I hated to look at myself and usually avoided my reflection at all costs. I had the worst acne. My skin was flaking and dry; I had rosacea; and my lips were gray, chapped, and raw. I looked unhealthy and unappealing in every way. Not only had my injury left me unable to move, it meant I could no longer regulate my ability to sweat, which meant that I had no way of flushing toxins from my pores. I was always trying to figure out if there was something new I could use to help tame my skin problems. At this point, I had bought and tried every product on the market. I'd sprung for the expensive miracle creams, the three-dollar pharmacy creams, and several prescription creams—all to no avail. Nothing worked, not even the three-hundred-dollar creams made from a four-star flower picked under the eighth rock on Mars. I still looked like Alf. Most of the products actually made my skin look worse, because I was so sensitive that I'd react badly to all kinds of different ingredients.

In desperation, my parents and I had begun experimenting with different essential oils, botanicals, natural remedies, and vitamin creams. My parents know pretty much everything there is to know about natural approaches to all kinds of health problems. They both regularly attend conferences to learn about progressive new approaches from Europe. Exasperated by the creams we were buying over the counter and getting on prescription, we began to have long conversations about what we could do for ourselves.

"Would lavender oil help with my skin?" I wanted to know.

"Well, it could be good, but it might irritate it; it might be too harsh," my dad advised.

"So what *could* I use?"

"Let's try some more aloe vera," my mom suggested. "Maybe if we put it in the fridge, it won't be so flaky."

Aloe vera is known for its healing properties, but in my case, it just wasn't strong enough. As soon as I put it on, it got sticky, and then when it dried, it flaked. Add this to my existing skin problems, and it was not a good look.

The skin on my face was the most glaring area of trouble, but it wasn't just my vanity that was spurring me to find a solution. I had skin problems all over. When you sit in a wheelchair all day long, you're constantly putting pressure on your skin, depriving it of oxygen, and limiting your blood circulation. I had breakouts over my entire body. This was dangerous. People who sit in wheel-chairs all day can easily develop sores. The sores can grow, then they can become infected, which can spread to your blood and to your heart. Which can be fatal. So you get pretty obsessed with your skin.

"There has to be something," I pointed out. "Maybe we just have to try something new. Or a combination of things."

I was aware that my parents' medical office is kept well supplied with all kinds of oils, botanicals, and extracts. They have two stock rooms, one in the basement and one behind reception, both filled with rows and rows of bottles, boxes, vials, and tubes of natural ingredients in their purest form—usually imported from Europe and therefore free of the kinds of artificial preservatives or fragrances that would inevitably irritate my skin.

My mom said she thought that was the way to go: combining ingredients that we thought might help, to see if this affected their potency. My dad quietly digested my questions and told me he'd get back to me.

First up, he gave me an unprocessed form of vitamin E to try. I was happy it didn't contain petroleum. Many skin creams that you find at the pharmacy or in department stores contain petrolatum, a petroleum by-product, which, I was discovering, acted like Saran Wrap, sitting on my skin rather than penetrating it, and clogging my pores even further. Since my accident, my sense of smell was heightened, so anything with petrolatum in it reeked of tar, as if I'd reached down and applied a big chunk of asphalt to my face. Which would be fine if it actually helped, but it didn't do anything except for putting a shiny, clogging smear on my already troubled skin.

"Let me know what you think, but I want to start trying some other vitamin extracts to see if they make any difference," my dad told me.

Vitamin E was greasy and it smelled like fish oil. Even if it might have been doing a little bit to help my skin, I didn't want to smell like sardines.

I began challenging my dad's knowledge: "How could we amplify the vitamin E by incorporating it with other ingredients?" I wanted to know. "What would happen if we mixed the vitamin E with calendula? Would it make the vitamin E more effective?" I'd had some success with calendula, which had proved to be very healing to my chapped lips, but even that wasn't enough. I needed something much stronger.

This is how it began. Mixing one thing with another.

"What happens if we mix the vitamin E with the aloe vera?" I wanted to know.

In fact, the vitamin E became less oily, and the aloe vera became less flaky. The aloe vera would dry down to a matte finish that helped with the oiliness of the vitamin E, without making my skin look worse.

Mixing creams became a new family obsession. Between my mom, my dad, and me, we started reading anything and everything that we could find on the subject of skin care. Often my parents ordered ingredients especially for me. Mostly, I would apply the raw oils and extracts directly to my face. Sometimes we would mix two ingredients in the palm of my hand before seeing how they would work on my skin. We were constantly reading more, testing new mixes, and asking questions. Over the coming months, we tried close to eighty different oils and creams on my face.

I was becoming my own lab rat.

I began to look online and subscribed to all the relevant medical journals. I read every article about skin care that I could get my hands on. After so many failures, I would find out about some new ingredient and wonder if it was even worth ordering it.

One day just before I left for Detroit, I was reading a medical journal and joking around with my sister.

"What do you think?" I asked. "If I close my eyes and then open this magazine, I will finally find the answer to all my problems."

"Go on, then," said Charlotte. "Play the lottery while you're at it. I can't wait for all to be revealed."

I closed my eyes and opened the magazine at a random page. When I opened my eyes, I was looking at an ad for a fiber supplement. OK, so that didn't work. But then I turned the page. Here I found a short write-up that described a naturally antibacterial, calming, and immunostimulating absolute essence of jasmine. Unlike essential oils, such essences are obtained from the residue left behind from the extraction of flower petals. It sounded like the fifty other essences I had already tried, but I decided to give it a go as a last resort. I asked my dad to order a raw version and began to apply it directly to my skin.

I first noticed the difference in Detroit. The weather in Michigan at that time of year was so cold and harsh that I assumed my skin would become cracked and dried, as it did in New York every winter. But this didn't happen. After about ten days of using the jasmine, my skin looked almost healthy. I stopped using the Jasmine Absolute for a couple of days and sure enough, my skin started cracking and drying out. I started using the Jasmine Absolute again. My skin began to get better.

"OK," said my dad when I got back from Detroit, "let's see what happens when we mix the jasmine with some of the other extracts and vitamins we've been trying."

When we combined the Absolute with various ingredients that had had a benign effect before, they began to show positive results. Not only did my hideous skin improve, over a period of days, it actually started to look not too bad.

"Wow, Francesco," my sister observed. "You're glowing. What's Dad putting in that concoction he's giving you? Because I want some. Now."

I gave Charlotte a vial to try.

A few days later she got back to me. "I need ten more. Today!" she told me. "Don't think you're going to keep this good stuff all for yourself." Even though my sister has naturally well-balanced skin, there was something about the jasmine that gave her an added boost. She looked as if she'd just gotten back from vacation.

Then my mom wanted in. After a few days, her skin felt softer and looked healthier. I felt pleased to be able to put a smile on her face. She worked so hard for me that it was great to be able to do something for her, for a change.

Suzan, who would visit me each week for our yoga and meditation session, quickly became addicted. Her skin is very sensitive and dry, but the jasmine rebalanced it. Pretty soon, I was getting panicked phone calls from my friend when she was running out and needed another vial.

"Is it me that you love, or only my jasmine?" I teased her.

"The jasmine, darling," she shot back. "You know I can't lie. . . ."

It turned out I had been an ideal lab rat. My skin is so sensitive and reacts to ingredients in such dramatic ways that I was the perfect litmus test for any ingredient that might be too harsh for anyone else. Equally, if the jasmine could rebalance *my* terrible skin, it seemed it might be able to work for anyone.

After my mom had been using the cream for a few weeks, I got a call from my dad's receptionist at the office.

"Um, you remember that vial you gave your mom?"

"Yes, what about it?"

"Well, can I have seven more?"

It turned out that patients at the office had been complimenting my mom on her newfound glow, and she'd been giving them samples to try. Already, about a half dozen patients were addicted. My dad treats many people who are undergoing chemotherapy, which can make skin extremely sensitive. The Jasmine Absolute was so gentle that it was ideal for them. People with allergies were also asking to try it, and some of the older women in the office—who'd noticed how my mom's wrinkles suddenly seemed less pronounced—wanted samples as well.

At first, that was as far as it went. I was just distributing the vials to family, friends, and my dad's patients. When you make your Christmas cookies and people ask for them, you don't think about opening up a pastry shop. But then the lightbulb went off. What if I started to market the jasmine cream? What if I started a skin-care line? Maybe this could be the outlet for my creativity and energy that I had been looking for. This might just be the key to my next step.

It didn't take me long to figure out a name for my new idea. Suzan was over for one of our regular yoga meditation sessions when I told her: "Guess what! I've decided to start a skin-care line. It's going to be called Clark's Botanicals."

"What?! That's great!"

"And I want to use the products to help people become aware about SCI and all the research that needs to get done."

"So does this mean I can finally buy what's in those vials?"

"Nah. I'll keep giving you your fix, don't worry." I was excited. This felt like the beginning.

Suzan was smiling. "This is going to be great. I know it."

This time, we skipped yoga; we had too much to talk about. Two hours flew by, and it felt like we'd hardly started. It would be difficult to go to sleep that night.

My parents came home around two a.m. from the office, and

my mother stopped by my room on her way to bed. That night, my mind was racing with ideas.

"I have a business idea," I told her. "I want to start Clark's Botanicals, a skin-care line."

"Good!" She didn't say much more at that moment, but I knew she was happy for me. At breakfast the next day, my dad's reaction was similar: "I think it's a great idea, Francesco." My parents acted as if this next chapter in my life was somehow inevitable: "Well, of course Francesco is going to start his own business. Why shouldn't he?" Their reaction helped give me the inner strength to forge ahead.

I knew that better skin was a huge confidence booster for me and I hoped I could do the same for others. When you look un-healthy, you can see the reaction in people's faces—they're pleased to see you, but at the same time, there's always that glimmer of concern in their eyes. I would register this, and it would make me shrink from making eye contact. Now when I met someone for the first time, I no longer avoided looking at them, and they no longer averted their eyes. For the first time since the accident, I was feeling confident and I had something to think about and talk about besides my injury and recovery. I was working with Mary and the committee. I was developing "my products." It felt good just to say that to people. I felt as if I was contributing. I wasn't a chemist, nor did I know how to cre-ate, market, and package products. I had no idea how I was go-ing to get my little vials into stores or magazines, or into people's homes. All I knew was that my skin had been in very bad shape and nothing on the market worked, and I wanted to change that.

As it turned out, the idea for the jasmine had been staring me in the face ever since China. While I'd been in the hospital in

Beijing, I'd drunk jasmine tea each day. Bird would serve endless cups of the stuff for its calming and healing properties. I'd been ingesting jasmine all that time without realizing that it held the key—not only to my skin problems, but also to what I was going to do with the next phase of my life.

23

What Do You Want to Do Today?

AFTER I RETURNED FROM DETROIT, I BEGAN TO ASK MYSELF A
simple question: What do you want to do today? It's the kind of
question able-bodied people ask themselves every day. What do
I want to eat? Who do I want to see? Where do I want to go?
How do I want to get there? But when you're injured in this way,
suddenly your life is no longer your own. You become completely
beholden to others—your family, your doctors, your therapists.
Sometimes, it's easy to forget that you're still an individual in
your own right. You go from having an independent existence,
living a life of your choice, to spending your whole time in a rehab hospital, pushing pennies into Play-Doh. For nearly three
years, I had spent every spare minute in therapy. I had put my
career and my personal and social life on hold. Three years later, I
knew I had to reclaim something for myself that was my own. Although the prospect of doing this was daunting, it was also liber-
ating to begin to think this way. Maybe I *could* make a new life for
myself, admittedly modified by my injury, but not totally defined
by it.

I got to work organizing my fund-raiser. I had just received money from an organization that awarded grants for people with disabilities, so I had some seed money to pay for converting the garage into a gym. But what I really wanted was a special exercise bicycle called the Giger MD that I had used in Detroit. I loved the feeling of being on the bike. It was set up so that I lay on my back with the pedals above me. There were pedals for my hands as well as my feet—I would turn the hand crank and it would help move my legs. When I was on the bike, I felt as if I was truly getting a workout and breaking a sweat. Not only did the bike help me maintain muscle strength, it would get my circulation going, which combats skin breakdown. I wanted to buy a Giger bike for my garage gym, but I needed to raise the money to do so. Until this point, I'd always resisted the idea of raising funds in this way. Reaching out to my friends and asking them for money would mean admitting that I needed help, and that was very hard for me to do. I never wanted anyone to feel sorry for me. I didn't want to appear to be in need. But the reality was that I did need help, and I began to realize that raising money was one way of assuming responsibility for the financial cost of my recovery. I also figured out that if I could find sponsors for the event—so that we would have food, drink, and prizes—then people would be getting something in return for their donations. I enlisted the help of my former boss from *Harper's Bazaar* and two other good friends from my magazine days to help me pull together the benefit. Suzan suggested calling the event "Francesco's Friends," and she created a website where people could donate money if they couldn't come. The whole thing snowballed. Suddenly, it wasn't just my friends who were helping out. Friends of friends of friends were also finding ways to contribute.

That night of the fund-raiser marked the end of my hibernation. At the party, I found myself out in the world again, surrounded by a large group of friends, and because everyone brought someone else, a whole lot of people I didn't even know. My skin was better. I felt better. I'd gotten rid of my paper pants, once and for all. I had my new business idea that I wanted to tell people about. I was back from China and back from Detroit, and I didn't just want to be in a therapy room anymore. I'd been in hiding, living someone else's life, imposed on me by my injury. I was out of practice at being in such a social setting, but in the end, I enjoyed myself.

"There's no way you have *this* many friends," my brother said soon after we arrived.

"Try me," I told him.

By the end of the evening, I had spoken to almost everyone in the room, and we had raised enough money for my bike.

Now that my home gym was set up, I could opt out of the hospital system completely. In Detroit I had seen how much I could achieve outside of the traditional physical-therapy model. There was no way I could go back to all those evaluations and restrictions again. I didn't want to spend my time trying to prove to my insurance company and my therapist that I needed to continue with therapy. At home, no one was telling me, "Oh, you can't do that because you've plateaued and your insurance won't cover it." Instead, I could focus on which modalities were *beneficial*. I was doing yoga stretches with one of my therapists, who would tailor the positions to my injury. I was pedaling my new bike. I was working my legs and my abs and my back. My therapy was designed to suit me and what I wanted to achieve. Best of all, therapy was no longer boring to me; I was working in ways that challenged me and that gave me a sense of progression.

"What do you want to do today?" This was the question I was asking myself, and my therapists were helping me to answer it.

The same question I was asking in therapy, I was also beginning to ask about the rest of my life. What did I want to do today? I knew I wanted to work again, and that I wanted to have my own business. I had no idea how I was going to take these creams that we were mixing at home and get them on the shelves of stores, but I was determined to figure out how to achieve this. For the rest of 2005, I worked with my dad on formulating a range of products, rather than just a single cream. As we'd done with the jasmine, we tested everything directly on my skin, the theory being that if it worked for me, it could work for anyone. Meanwhile, we continued to sell the original cream to our growing number of customers who came to it purely by word of mouth. We had a Clark family cottage industry going. There was no design to the packaging. My mom and my sister would sit for hours, mixing the ingredients, sticking labels on jars, filling them with the cream, then screwing on lids. As a business, it was self-sustaining. The creams paid for themselves, but it wasn't like we were making any money. It was truly a labor of love for all involved.

I obsessed over the new formulations for the creams and balms until I knew them forward, backward, and inside-out. I pored over the ingredients every day, looking over pages and pages of ideas divided into three lists: "No-No Ingredients," "Definitely Yes Ingredients," and "Goals." My father's ear was stretched beyond its limits with my questions about homeopathy, vitamins, and botanical extracts, and how to incorporate his learning into everything I did. I decided I wanted to make a lip balm because my lips had been constantly chapped and cracked since my accident. Regular lip balms on the market just made my lips greasy, without actually helping them to heal. I was still very sensitive to smell, and because the balms had petrolatum in them, I would find the smell of tar overpowering.

"I don't want a lip balm that smells like asphalt," I told my dad.

"OK, so we'll try shea butter instead of petrolatum as the base," my dad suggested.

We tried, but the new balm ended up as hard as rock.

"We could use sweet almond oil. It should soften the balm," my dad suggested.

We tried again. The next version of the balm looked as if it was sweating. My dad basically presented me with a pot of waxy oil.

"We can't market that," I pointed out. "I don't even want to put it on myself!"

We had to get the shea butter to act like petrolatum, with that same smooth consistency. We wanted to add ingredients like calendula that would help my lips to heal. We didn't want to use any artificial preservatives. By the fifth version, we weren't even close. This mixture was gritty, as if we'd shaken sand into it. I started buying every lip balm on the market, compulsively reading the ingredients lists to try to figure out how they worked. After twenty-six versions of our lip-balm recipe, it looked like we'd done it. The balm had a nice rich texture, and when I applied it to my lips, it started working right away, healing the broken skin. Sadly, after a few weeks, the beeswax in the mixture started to crystallize. The balm was ruined. We had to start all over again. I was beginning to understand why people used petrolatum as a base for these products. It would have been so much easier, but even so, I was determined to find some other way.

On the twenty-seventh try, we got it. This version of the lip balm worked perfectly.

As the year went on, I was feeling more comfortable about the products in general. I was ready to find a factory to mix the formulations and manufacture them for me, so I started to do my research. These weren't the kinds of places you could look up in the Yellow Pages. I must have spoken to dozens of people before I even found a phone number. I called that first factory and got a resounding "no." Perhaps this shouldn't have been surprising. We were completely unknown. We had hardly any money. We had nowhere to sell the products. Most factories work with the big names, the Lauders, the Ardens, the L'Oréals—companies that want many hundreds of thousands of units manufactured. I was still thinking in dozens, not thousands. I was smaller than small-fry. I contacted twenty factories before I found a reputable company that would take me on.

At the beginning of 2006, and after months of work, I was finally ready to begin working with the factory on making the products. I put up the small amount of money I'd made from the creams so far, maxed out my credit cards, and borrowed money from my parents. This was scary. This wasn't just some little pet project anymore; it was becoming a real business. While things were starting to take shape, I was painfully aware that I was an absolute beginner. I was going to be working with chemists on these formulations, but it wasn't like I had a background in science. My lack of knowledge inspired me to become a student of every ingredient, researching each one, learning everything there was to know about them. The list of ingredients for each product was at least three pages long. I would wake up at three a.m. remembering something extra or something I wanted to take out of the mix. With every passing day I was sharpening my memory— something common to many people who are unable to write information down.

Three months after I signed up with the factory, the product samples began arriving. Although I had sent the chemists the same list of ingredients and percentages that I had developed with my dad, in the setting of a factory lab, everything came out differently. The glycolic acid was reacting badly with one of the vitamins we were using. The odor of the green tea in one of the products was too strong. I couldn't find the quantity of French algae that I needed for the body wash—it was going to take four months to grow and harvest enough to manufacture even the smallest amount. The factory samples went back and forth as I tested them, tweaked the percentages, and made further suggestions. Every day I was on the phone to the factory. I got to know the chemists very well in that time. They understood that this wasn't your usual business venture; I wasn't in it for the money. I was doing this because I wanted to make something that would help people, in the same way I had managed to help myself.

As the products began to improve, I was ready to find another factory to make the packaging. This turned out to be just as frustrating and time-consuming as developing the formulations. I wanted the plastic bottles to look like old glass, the kind you find in an apothecary. When I tried to communicate this to the factory, they looked at me as if I were speaking Greek. I realized I needed to learn to be descriptive, while still keeping it simple. I wanted the design to be unisex, to look interesting and elegant. Many hours were spent poring over Pantone colors and fonts. I wanted the jars to reflect the fact that the products were natural, but without putting them in recycled brown cardboard with a hemp bow. We were going with dark green bottles with big, white letters, in a font that was drawn by hand. Above all, I wanted the look of the products to reflect all the thought and care that had gone into them. I wanted them to look *smart*.

By now, I was completely invested in this project. It was so important to me that Clark's Botanicals did well. The purpose of the products was to raise awareness for the search for a cure, but there was even more at stake. Every bottle and jar was the sum of my story: my injury, my dad's expertise and patience, all those hours my mom and sister had spent filling jars and sticking on labels. So much belief and goodwill. I just hoped that I could make something of this business, because it had already become my overriding passion.

24

~~~~

Connecting the Dots

AT TIMES, IT FELT AS IF I'D LIVED TWO LIVES, AS IF THERE WAS my life before my accident and then my life afterward. Before the accident I was studying, working, trying to make a success of myself. In the split second of my accident, my life ended and another life began. It wasn't just my spine that was severed—I was completely cut off from my existence as I used to know it. I was forced to start again from a point somewhere below zero. I had to learn how to breathe on my own, how to hold my head on my shoulders; I had to learn how to sit up, how to move my arms, how to operate within a set of extreme limitations. It was hard. Everything that I had achieved before my accident had become worthless. All the investment of love and money from my parents to put me through school and college; all my hard work to graduate from college and pursue a career; what did I have to show for it? For a long time, my accident seemed to cancel out my life that had gone before it. I couldn't deal with the present, so I just wanted to live in the past. I had been locked in time, unable to move ahead.

But now I was further down the line, I realized that I didn't have to split my story into two anymore. Everything that came before my injury—my upbringing, my studies, my interests, my work—all of this was giving me a strong foundation on which to build my new life.

One day in the summer of 2006, my pre-injury and post-injury lives came together for the first time. I was in the van with my sister, heading toward Manhattan, going back to *Harper's Bazaar* to meet with the editors there. By this time, I had the products in their smart new bottles in my hands. If they weren't completely finished, then they were very close. The week before I'd e-mailed Glenda Bailey, the magazine's editor in chief, updating her on my progress and letting her know about Clark's Botanicals. She responded right away, suggesting that I meet with the beauty director of the magazine to tell her about what I was doing. I knew from working at the magazine that the editors at *Bazaar* had the highest of standards. They were accustomed to working with Chanel, Dior, Yves Saint Laurent—the biggest names in the business. Meanwhile, my desk in my bedroom was cluttered with glass and plastic bottles, no labels, no boxes, still filled with the almost-finished formulations. I went into overdrive. I was on the phone with the factory, the bottle designer, the person who was helping with graphics and a website. I must have used all of my monthly cell-phone minutes in one day. But it was worth it. By the time my sister and I were on our way to the meeting, we were bringing with us an elegant one-page summary describing how it all began, a catalogue, and all of the products in their crisp new bottles.

In the van, I was jittery with nerves. I had been back to the office a year before, just to say hi and to tell people I was thinking about starting a skin-care line. Now there was much more at stake. Clark's Botanicals wasn't a hobby. I was trying to break into the beauty business and raise awareness for a cure all at the same time. I needed to see if I could get the support of some of

the most important people in magazines; and because these were
my former colleagues, their approval meant the world to me. As
we entered the lobby and went up in the elevator, I tried to remain calm. The magazine had moved into a new building by this
time, so everything felt unfamiliar, which added to my nervous-
ness. Glenda's assistant greeted me at the elevator, then two of
the fashion editors I used to work with came over to say hello and
catch up, helping to put me at ease.

First, I went in to see Alexandra Parnass, *Bazaar*'s beauty director.
She had arrived at *Bazaar* after I'd left, so we quickly calculated
how narrowly we'd missed meeting each other before.

"So, tell me about Clark's Botanicals," she began.

I started to tell her my story. As I described each one of the
products, Alexandra was closely examining the ingredients, the
packaging, the consistency of the creams. I hoped they were going
to pass the test. She began applying different lotions to the back of
her hand and sniffing each one, like a connoisseur with wine.

"I really love what you're doing with the line," she told me.
"But what are you going to do if it takes off and a store wants it,
and suddenly you need eight thousand units?"

I didn't have an answer to that question yet, but even so, it
sounded like a pretty good problem to have. I figured I'd probably cross that bridge when I got to it.

As the meeting was drawing to a close, Glenda came into the
room.

"Francesco!" she exclaimed, giving me a kiss on the cheek. "I
hear you have a fabulous new skin-care line."

Her familiar English accent reminded me that she wasn't a
stranger. I was very happy to see her.

"I have the funniest story to tell you," she said, and she launched
into a juicy anecdote about a certain British celebrity. This immediately put me at ease, as she knew it would.

"So, tell me about Clark's Botanicals," she prompted.

I started talking about the products again, and Glenda began to dab some of the eye cream around her eyes.

"Everyone could always use a good eye cream," she pointed out. She told me she liked the font on the packaging, the bold green bottles. She was wearing the same shade of green that day. I couldn't have planned it if I'd tried.

I remembered well all the hours spent in editorial meetings with Glenda, learning so much from her sure sense of vision, her grasp of every detail. Being back in the office reminded me how much I loved working in the magazine world. I loved the excitement and the energy. I had met such dynamic people through my work, and helped to create a product that I took pride in. Now Clark's Botanicals was offering me a way of reconnecting with my past life; a way of using what I'd learned from people like Glenda and bringing it to bear upon my new business. It was very much a feeling of connecting the dots of past and present.

As we said our good-byes, I wasn't sure what impact I'd made on the editors at *Bazaar*; I just hoped that we'd begun some kind of dialogue. Besides, something else good came out of my visit to the office that day.

As I was finishing chatting with Glenda, Stephen Gan, the magazine's creative director, came out to say hi. He hadn't seen me since my injury, and wanted to catch up.

"Francesco, it's so good to see you," he said. "Let's get a drink at the coffee machine and you can tell me what's been going on."

Charlotte came and joined us, and Stephen immediately began joking with her about the time I had embarrassed myself at the office Halloween karaoke party.

"There's your brother, dressed like a cowboy, singing Madonna's 'Don't Stop.'" Stephen laughed.

"You can laugh," Charlotte told him. "I have to live with this every day."

At this point, I happened to mention to Stephen that I had been planning to book tickets to see Madonna for Charlotte for her birthday.

"But I left it too late," I said. "Madonna's only playing two nights in New York, and they're both totally sold out."

The next day, I got a call from Stephen's assistant. He had managed to get us two tickets to see Madonna that coming Friday. Front-row seats at Madison Square Garden! When I told Charlotte the news, she ran around the room, her arms waving in the air. "What am I going to wear?" she screamed. Charlotte is usually pretty calm and composed, but now she was actually giddy.

Friday came, and we drove back into town together for the second time that week. It felt great to be doing something that was so much fun and that was making my sister so happy. The past four years had been hard on her, and I knew how many sacrifices she had made on my behalf. She had stayed on at home, at a time when most of her friends were moving away, so that she could look after me while my mom was at work. Charlotte had spent hours of her life driving me around to meetings and rehab hospitals. She had traveled to China and stayed with me there even after my mother came back. It was true she wanted to be a doctor, but even so, she was a young woman at a point in her life when she should be taking flight, and instead she was stuck at home with her brother in a wheelchair. Although it must have been difficult for her at times, I never got the sense that she resented any of this. It was her instinct to help me. So if anyone deserved to have a great night out, it was Charlotte.

When we arrived at Madison Square Garden, we made our way through the gathering crowds and into the arena to find our seats. We were excited to sit in the front row, but when we got to our allocated seats, we realized that our view was completely blocked by the people who had run to the front of the stage and who were standing right in front of us. Sitting in a wheelchair, I couldn't see a thing.

"Just go up to the stage, like everyone else, once the show starts," said one of the women sitting next to us.

As the lights dimmed, we did that, but I was nearly knocked out of my chair by more people rushing the stage. It was like a mob. The fire marshal came over, telling us that we had to move because we were a fire hazard. We were given new seats. Then a security guard came and moved us again. Before I knew it, someone else was moving us again. No one knew what to do with us. We must have been moved five times.

"Put me in the last row in the last seat," I told the security guy, "but just don't move me again."

Finally, a guy in a baseball cap who was sitting in the front row saw what was going on.

"Why don't you come sit with me and I'll just move over? There's an empty seat next to me."

My sister looked at him, and her jaw dropped. "Oh my God, it's Leo. Hi, Leo!"

It was Leonardo DiCaprio. He was sitting in the front row, right at the end of the catwalk that extended out into the audience, and there was no one standing in front of that area.

"You'll be able to see from here," he pointed out.

As the show began, Madonna was literally ten feet in front of us. It was such a spectacle that for those brief hours, I didn't feel like I was injured at all. I didn't feel like I was in a wheelchair. I was just having fun, pure and simple. It was a fantastic night. As the show ended, Leonardo shook my hand and we exchanged a couple of words. Others had ignored our situation, and he could have done the same, but he chose not to and I appreciated that.

The next day, I sent Leo some Clark's Botanicals products to say thank you. I also e-mailed Arianne Phillips, Madonna's stylist. This was the same person who had set up my call with Madonna at Mount Sinai Hospital immediately after my accident. I told Arianne that I couldn't think of a better way to spend an evening than watching Madonna in concert. Arianne replied, telling me she'd forwarded my e-mail to Madonna. A few days later I got another e-mail from Arianne including a note from Madonna.

"Yes, I remember speaking with Francesco at Mount Sinai," Madonna wrote. "I saw him sitting next to Leo at Madison Square Garden. He was wearing a black shirt. It certainly sounds like he's making something of his life."

That same week, I sent Madonna some of my products as a token of appreciation. I wanted her to know that her call to me at Mount Sinai had lifted my spirits at one of the lowest points of my life. Arianne soon e-mailed and said that Madonna loved the products, and that she thanked me for sending them over.

It was a week of good e-mails. The beauty team at *Bazaar* also got in contact. They were going to feature my products for an upcoming issue. Clark's Botanicals was going to be thrust into the public eye—this was no longer just for friends and family. We weren't even sold anywhere yet beyond my bedroom; but we were on our way.

25

Twenty-Nine

BEFORE I KNEW IT, IT WAS FEBRUARY, AND MY TWENTY-ninth birthday was just a few days away. It had been nearly five years since my injury and almost three years since my trip to China. Yes, I had seen progress, and I had gotten so much stronger. I could use my arms and hands, to an extent. I was able to kick my legs with a large amount of effort. I spent every day on my bike in my gym. I could sit up at the edge of my bed. But this wasn't enough; I wanted to *keep* making progress. More than anything, I feared hitting a plateau or even regressing. How far had I come since this time last year? What did I have to show for all the work I had done with my therapists? I didn't enjoy this feeling of my recovery slipping out of my control. Yet another year of my life had gone by, and I was still stuck in this chair.

I decided to do something to help me feel good about my birthday. I wanted to make a resolution. On the day of my birthday, I was going to set a goal for myself. Something new, something I hadn't done before. And I was going to make this commitment to myself every year, so that maybe this way I wouldn't have to dread

February coming around anymore. The day of my twenty-ninth birthday, I decided I wanted to find another research trial that was going on and get involved. Two years had gone by since I'd participated in the treadmill study at Kessler. I was long overdue to try something new. On the day of my birthday, I picked up the phone and called Burke, and the rehabilitation department that I had attended there. I wanted to know if they were doing any new SCI research or if they knew of anyone else who was conducting work in the field.

One of my former therapists answered the phone and recognized my name and voice immediately. I told her why I was calling.

"Actually, I'm really happy you called us," she told me. "We have a new research study happening right here and now."

In turned out that the researchers at the Burke-Cornell Medical Research Institute were using robots to help people regain mobility in their arms. She gave me the number for the department, and I called it right away. One of the research assistants answered, and by pure coincidence, it turned out that they had an opening. Two weeks later I was going to have an initial evaluation.

It wasn't until I went to meet the researchers a couple of weeks later that I found out I was the first person with a spinal-cord injury to participate in the study. Until now, they had been working exclusively with stroke patients who had lost sensation in their arms. Now they were keen to find out what kinds of results they would see on someone with SCI.

The first person I met was Dr. Victor, who was overseeing the study.

"What we plan to do with you, Francesco," said Dr. Victor, "is to look at how the brain, the spinal cord, and muscle function interrelate in a spinal-cord patient working with our interactive robotic devices." He explained at great length what they hoped to achieve. "We're seeing a growing amount of anecdotal evidence that appears to indicate that it is possible to use the plasticity of the spinal cord to help promote neural regeneration in SCI patients," he told me. What they were hoping was that by working with me, they could corroborate this.

It was as if Dr. Victor was a gourmet chef describing how he was going to make the most delicious chocolate soufflé. Meanwhile, I'd been hungry for hours, and just wanted to eat.

"So what you're saying is that I can get better?" I asked.

"Well, yes. We just need to demonstrate and document that."

I was one step ahead in my mind. I was *certain* that my spinal cord was able to regenerate. Now I wanted the scientists to get on board. I wanted Dr. Victor and his team to skip to the next stage, the part where doctors and researchers would actually begin to figure out how we could promote more of this regeneration.

That day, I was given a baseline evaluation. This consisted of various tests. I had to close my eyes and touch the tip of my nose with my left hand. I had to pick up pennies and try to lift a full bottle of water. I had to pick up nine poker chips and stack them one on top of the other. Then I was asked to flip over all the playing cards in a pack. Everything I did was timed with a stopwatch.

I began going to Burke-Cornell twice a week, for two and a half hours, for the next eight months. I became good friends with the research assistants, and I would bring them CD mixes to play during our sessions. Each session began with one of the assistants meticulously strapping my arm inside a robotic arm. Then they turned on the computer and I did my first test run. In front of me was a computer screen, displaying a circle shape that looked like a dartboard, with little colored dots that would appear around its outer rim. I had to move a joystick so that the cursor would go from the center of the circle and touch each of the dots. The first time, I did this without any assistance from the robot. The researchers showed me a visual depiction of the motions I had made: It was less a pattern and more a jagged scrawl. Obviously I was going to have to work on this. Next I had to do the same exercise, but with the help of the robot. Whenever I was unable to move my hand and arm on my own, the robot would sense that I had stalled, and it would give me the smallest nudge to help me to move again. It was as if the robot was replicating the normal brain-body connection that I lacked. I did this exercise over and over again, getting through three sets in every session. Each set meant moving the cursor onto the dots 360 times. It was tedious and repetitive work, but because the robot was helping me achieve this in such a subtle, precise, and consistent way, it was helping me build new muscular control in my arms.

As the months went on, Dr. Victor and his assistants continued to do regular evaluations. I did my tricks with the pennies, the blocks, the cards, and the bottle of water all over again. I just wanted to prove to the doctors that this was working, that I could do this. And I was seeing improvements. For the first time since my accident, I could straighten out my arms: The muscles were no longer tight and contracted from lack of use. I could use my triceps. It felt as if there was a little worm jiggling around in my upper arm, the muscle was so weak and flimsy, but even so, I was feeling it.

One of the biggest changes I saw was my ability to flip my hands over both ways, to pronate and supernate my hands. This had been impossible for me before. I could flip my hand up, but I could never flip my hand down. In order to flip my hand down, I would have to pick up my elbow and throw it so that my arm would flail my hand in the right direction. Now that I could flip both ways, I was so excited, I would flip over and over again. This was always my instinct when I got back new muscle; I just wanted to use it, to prove that I could, but also to build up the muscle. For the first time since my accident, I could slowly reach my arm forward, controlling the movement, rather than having to throw my arm out in front of me. This made many new things possible.

One evening, I was eating dinner. My mom had made french fries, and I dropped one off my plate. Then I picked it up and put it in my mouth. I didn't think about it. I just did it.

"Wait, what did you just do?" my mom asked.

"Do it again!" Charlotte cried.

Normally, in order to pick up the french fry, I would have to throw my arm out in front of me so that I could use my whole hand to shovel the french fry back toward me, as if I were using a rake. Now I was able to extend my arm out in the direction of the object and actually use my thumb and index finger to pick up it up. I'm not saying I have the same fine motor control I had before my accident. I'm still clumsy, and often have to use my hand and fist, rather than my fingers, to move something toward me. To most people, it probably wouldn't look like I'd achieved much. But compared to the zero mobility I'd had before, the improvement meant the world. For me, being able to use my hands and fingers is the difference between dependence and independence. If I had full use of my hands, I could manage to live alone.

At the end of the study, the doctor and assistants told me they were planning to develop new robots for fingers, ankles, and legs. I told them to sign me up for any new trial in the future. They agreed with me that I had regained movement that I did not have at the beginning of the study. Something was happening, something that I had been told so many times was completely impossible.

"Francesco, your neurons appear to be regenerating," Dr. Victor told me. "And to be honest with you, my colleagues and I have never seen anything like this before."

The New Sensation

"SO WHY WOULD ANYONE BUY THIS CRAP?"

It was spring of 2007 and I was in a meeting with a business mentor who was supposed to be going over the business plan for Clark's Botanicals. I'd applied for a New York State grant for start-up companies, and one of the requirements was that you had to meet with a businessperson who would evaluate your plan before you could be awarded the grant.

"I don't know if anyone's going to buy it," I replied. "But I know it's good, and it works. We're at a point where we're getting featured in magazines and we have a lot of retail interest, but I don't have any investors. With the money I receive from this grant, I'm going to start manufacturing and doing PR."

My mentor was recently retired from the insurance business. Through no fault of his own, it was clear he knew absolutely nothing about the beauty industry. So he had decided to play tough cop instead. I had already spent most of the meeting trying to educate him about what the difference was between an eye cream and a facial moisturizer. I was growing frustrated, and now he was calling my products "crap." My mentor put on his reading glasses and leaned back in his chair. Then he lowered his glasses.

"So what exactly do you know about skin care?" he wanted to know.

"Absolutely nothing," I told him. "But that doesn't mean I can't learn. In fact, I already have."

"Good answer," he said. The tough-cop thing was obviously his shtick. Even so, I wished he'd had some insight into what I was trying to do.

"We started out with a boutique in Bronxville, my hometown," I told him. "Now we're going to be sold in C.O. Bigelow and Henri Bendel in New York and Fred Segal in Los Angeles." It was a slow process, but after a lot of hard work and many meetings, we had gotten Clark's Botanicals into some pretty major stores.

"Henri who?"

"Bendel. You know. The department store on Fifth Avenue in New York."

"Hmm. Have you thought about Walgreens?"

"If I wanted to be sold in Walgreens, I would have to get investors so I could actually buy enough product to meet that kind of distribution need," I explained to him. "For the moment, I'm sticking to smaller stores and growing little by little."

It was as if I was giving him an education in how to start a skin-care line, not the other way around. Even so, I was aware that if I could convince this guy that Clark's Botanicals was a good idea, then I could convince anyone.

"What do you have that makes you competitive in this market?"

"I think our first advantage is that we started from scratch, so we've managed to create something unique. I didn't know anything about how to do this when I started, which is why I know more about the whole process than many experienced chemists. I had to do my research on every single ingredient and find out how they interacted with each other. If I tried an ingredient and my skin didn't look good, we reworked the formulation. Our goal is always to have a great product that really works."

My mentor was quiet. He took off his glasses and he put the products down on the table.

Silence.

"Anything else that makes you different?" he finally asked.

"Well, for one thing, we have no methylparaben, or any paraben preservatives in our products. Parabens are a great way to keep your beauty products fresh for many years, but studies have shown that parabens have led to elevated levels of estrogen, possibly causing breast cancer . . ."

Suddenly, in the middle of my spiel, the strangest thing happened. I was uncomfortable. Why was I uncomfortable? What was going on? Wait a minute. I could feel my butt! Holy shizzle mizzle! I just got back the sensation in my butt in the middle of this crazy meeting. I started to wiggle around in my seat; I needed to get out of that wheelchair. I felt as if I had been sitting in coach on a twenty-hour flight and needed to get up and stretch my legs. It hurt! But even so, the pain made me smile like a madman. In the past, I had sometimes felt a dull pins-and-needles sensation in my backside when I'd been sitting for a long time, but this was different. This was 100 percent feeling! I was sitting, and I could *feel* it. Bam! Just like that, it was back.

"Your business plan looks good," my mentor told me, oblivious to the fact that lightning had struck, right there in front of him. "Let's talk some more about your competitors."

Huh? I couldn't listen to a word he was saying. He must have thought I was insane. I was grinning from ear to ear. I was jubilant; I was ecstatic. I was getting better!

"Are you OK?" he asked. "Is everything all right?"

"Yes! I just got back feeling in my butt!" I blurted out. "And I'm in an incredible amount of pain!" I started to laugh. I had been waiting for something like this to happen for five years, and it had finally taken place in the middle of a business meeting with a complete stranger. Such is life.

"Wow. That's . . . really, well, I suppose that's good news," he said. I couldn't tell if he was smiling or frowning.

"Yes, yes it is," I replied. "Look, I hate to cut our meeting short, but I need to go." I looked down at my cell phone to see what time it was. Whoa. We had been in that room for three and a half hours. No wonder my butt hurt.

I said my good-byes. I needed to get home so I could get out of my chair and into my standing frame. I needed the pain to go away. On the way home, I was beaming and intoning *"owwwwww"* at the same time. The minute I got home, I called out to my mother.

"Mom!"

"How did the meeting go?" she asked, coming out of the kitchen.

"I can feel my butt!"

"What do you mean, you can feel your butt?" she asked.

"I mean, it hurts! And I can feel it!"

Then she got it.

"Yay! That's amazing!" She was cheering.

"I feel like I just sat through *The English Patient* four times without being able to move from my seat!"

"Yay!"

"I'm going to go nuts if I sit here a minute longer! I have to stand up!"

We carried on clapping and cheering all the way to the garage and my standing frame. My new sensation was excruciating and intoxicating at the same time. After standing for a few minutes, the pain subsided and I could relax again. From now on, I would have an indicator if I had been sitting for too long: pain. Amazing. I couldn't take it in. Could I really feel my butt? Yes, there it was, right there where it had always been.

At first, I was probably experiencing about 30 percent in terms of intensity of feeling. But then, little by little, I kept getting more and more feeling back, until I was probably at about 70 percent. The good part was that I could now feel when I needed to shift in my seat. Before, all I knew was that I was sweating like crazy—my body's way of alerting me that there was a problem. Now I knew when I had to shuffle in my seat or go and lie down or stand in my standing frame. On the downside, if the pain came on and I was out of the house, I would just have to grit my teeth. This was annoying—literally a pain in the ass—but even so, I would rather have the pain, because it was a clear message from my body. Pain told me I had to do something to fix a problem, and so I would fix it. I loved having that clarity back.

My doctors from Burke-Cornell didn't know what to say about my regained sensation. The conventional wisdom is that SCI patients sometimes see improvements like these in the first year or so after injury as the swelling in the spine goes down. But I was five years down the line. The doctors couldn't tell me if it was from the Chinese surgery, my daily five-hour therapy regimen, the robotic training, or just my body repairing itself. They performed more surface EMG tests on me, and these came back positive. Without a doubt, my muscles were working and reacting.

I had been seeing a neurologist once a year since my injury, to monitor my progress. When I went for my annual checkup in the summer, he was at a loss for words. The level of sensation that I was currently experiencing had dropped five vertebrae. My sensation level at the time of my accident was C4—around the fourth cervical vertebra at the back of my neck. After my China surgery, that dropped to C6—two vertebrae below my initial level. By the time I finished the robotic arm study, I had come down to the level of my T1 vertebra, which is the first thoracic vertebra located below the neck.

"Honestly, I've never seen a recovery like this," the neurologist told me. "When we see a degree of recovery with these injuries, it's usually in the first year. But you've been injured for five years. I don't know what it is you're doing that's working. But whatever it is, I suggest that you keep doing it."

It's my belief that it's the combination of everything I've done and continue to do that helps me to recover. The surgery has obviously helped me to regain sensation, but without the therapy to rebuild my muscles, the surgery would have been pointless. It's impossible to single out one factor and say, "That's what's working," because if I took one element out of the mix, then it would probably affect all the other elements.

As it turned out, Clark's Botanicals was highly recommended by my business mentor friend. One month after my meeting with him, I found out that I had received the small-business grant from New York State. The next stage of the plan for the business could now get under way.

27

The Reeve Foundation

CLARK'S BOTANICALS WAS BEGINNING TO GET ATTENTION IN the press, and I knew that I wanted to use this opportunity to create more awareness about the search for a cure. Every time a magazine reporter contacted me, I would tell them the story of my injury and my recovery. In some small way, I was helping to get the word out, but I wanted to do more. I wanted to donate a percentage of Clark's Botanicals profits to SCI research, and I wanted to do this through the Reeve Foundation. The Reeve Foundation had been the first place we'd contacted after my injury, and the advice and support we'd received at that time had been a lifeline. Ever since then, I'd been visiting the Reeve Foundation website on a daily basis. I'd go there for news updates and to learn about grants, new treatments, and research trials that were coming up. Although Christopher and Dana Reeve had both passed on, the organization they had founded continued to be instrumental in funding and advocating for the most innovative research going on in the country. I revered the foundation, and I had been waiting to get to a point with my company where

I felt confident that I had something to give back to an organization that had done so much for me.

Through a friend, I was introduced to one of the original founders of the Stifel Paralysis Foundation, which later evolved into the Reeve Foundation. We met for coffee in the spring of 2007, and I told this friend of a friend about Clark's Botanicals and how I hoped to contribute to the Reeve Foundation in some way. She told me that she would see what she could do. I later got an e-mail to say she was going to put me in touch with Peter Wilderotter, the Reeve Foundation's president and CEO.

The next day, I was working at my desk when the phone rang. I didn't recognize the number, but I picked up. It was Mr. Wilderotter, calling to introduce himself. He immediately began asking me questions about my injury and my recovery, and about Clark's Botanicals. I briefly told him my story. Then Mr. Wilderotter asked if he could come and meet me in person.

"I'll come up to Bronxville," he promised. "When works best for you?"

"Um, when works best for you?" I asked. "I'll make sure I'm here, believe me."

It was one of those phone calls where you hang up and wonder, Did that really just happen?

A few days later, Mr. Wilderotter arrived for his visit, forty-five minutes early. My mother was a nervous wreck. She must have cleaned the house five times already that morning. Now Mr. Wilderotter was here early, and she hadn't boiled the kettle for the tea yet; she hadn't laid out the cookies! She was so overwhelmed that after she introduced herself, she was at a loss for words, which is definitely not like my mother. For both of us, the Reeve Foundation was the apotheosis, and that made Mr. Wilderotter something like a deity.

That afternoon, I told Mr. Wilderotter some more about my

story, how the business began and how it had grown, and about going to China. I had the feeling I was auditioning for a part, even though I didn't know exactly what my role was. As I spoke, Mr. Wilderotter quietly listened to me.

Then he asked me, "So how can we help you, Francesco?"

"Honestly, I just want to participate in the foundation and contribute in any way I can," I told him.

Mr. Wilderotter left, promising that he would be in contact very soon.

A few weeks later I found myself on my way to Short Hills, New Jersey, to the Reeve Foundation headquarters. Mr. Wilderotter had arranged for me to meet the team who ran the organization. Although I had no idea exactly what was in store for me, I did know that I was very excited to visit the foundation and meet the people who worked there.

As I entered the lobby, the first thing I saw was an empty wheelchair. I knew right away whose this was, and it stopped me in my tracks. The chair looked so much smaller now, diminished and almost inconsequential without him. It was Mr. Reeve who had made the chair seem imposing with the sheer force of his presence.

"Francesco, hi, so happy to see you." Patricia Stush, one of the foundation's directors, came over to greet me. "I've got you doughnuts and coffee; and tea and water and soda."

She was warm and engaging, and offering me food. Of course, I liked her right away.

Patricia led me toward a conference room, with a glass wall facing the reception area. One by one, people who worked at the Reeve Foundation began arriving at the meeting, coming over to say hello. When the meeting began, Patricia introduced everyone. The department heads and their teams had prepared a Power-Point presentation about their role in the organization to show me. They were a dynamic bunch, of all ages and from all back-grounds. There were scientists, businesspeople, communications people, social workers, computer people, and educators, and they were bringing all those skills to bear on their work for the organization. Each person who presented seemed more enthusiastic and accomplished than the last.

The head of research talked me through all of the data that he had accumulated over the past year, drawing on the many research studies that the foundation was currently funding and monitoring. The PR team presented their work, which included organizing and promoting the foundation's annual gala. The education team spoke about the incredible archive of resources they had accumulated about SCI. I had already benefited from this service: After my injury, when my mother had called the foundation, the education department had sent her a wealth of information about insurance, medical facts, and upcoming research projects.

In the first place, I couldn't believe that this impressive presentation was really for my benefit. What could I bring to the table that was going to be just as important and effective? What could I do to further this cause? After I left that day, I felt energized. I had just met with a group of people who were extremely smart, engaged, and inspiring. They made me want to do more, to figure out how I could contribute in any way possible.

A few days later, I was pedaling on my bike in the garage when I got a call from the organization's director.

"Francesco," she said, "we'd like to ask you to become a National Ambassador for the Reeve Foundation. I'm calling to see whether this is something you'd be interested in doing."

Interested? For a second, all I could say was "Wow." Then I answered, "Yes, I'd be honored!"

Patricia took the time to tell me about the other ambassadors, nine in total, some able-bodied, some paralyzed, all from different backgrounds, but everyone committed to bringing attention to the many issues surrounding SCI.

"Actually, there's something else," said Patricia. "We were also wondering if you'd be interested in starting a new committee with Alexandra and Matthew Reeve, Christopher Reeve's son and daughter, to help draw younger members to the organization."

"Yes, definitely. I'd love to," I said. "Of course!"

After I hung up, I tried to absorb what had just happened. It was one of those moments when I was so thankful for my mother and my father. Ever since I was a baby, they'd surrounded me with the love, support, and guidance I needed to grow—and never more so than since my accident. Right from the beginning, they'd taught me the importance of learning and asking questions, of being an active participant in the world. Their expectation after my injury was that I would continue to work hard, just as I'd done before my accident, and that I would keep improving. Their quiet belief in me gave me the reason to get up each morning and go on. I knew that everything they had done for me had led me to this point.

My mom was at work already that day, and so I called the doctor's office.

"Mom, I'm going to be a National Ambassador," I told her. "For the Reeve Foundation."

Suddenly I heard some fumbling and then silence.

"Mom?"

"Checco, I just dropped the phone!"

"They're starting a committee called the Champions Committee, and we have to start planning the next event. We're meeting in a month."

"Well, I must say they made a very good choice," said my mother, who had regained her control of the telephone.

"*Grazie mille, Mamma,*" I told her. A thousand thanks.

My dad's response was to give me one of his rare compliments. "Well done, Francesco, I'm proud of you."

My mom later told me that he spent the next month telling every single patient at the office that I'd been "appointed ambassador."

The following February, I helped put together my first event for the Reeve Foundation. I had been planning a launch party for Clark's Botanicals around that time, and now that I was involved with the foundation, it made sense to turn the event into a fundraiser. What's more, it was nearly my birthday. The year before, I'd promised myself that I would always start something new with each birthday. This year's resolution was to pour my energies into working with the Reeve Foundation.

The night of the fund-raiser was a convergence of friends, family, foundation members, magazine people, and friends of friends. This was the first time I met Alexandra and Matthew Reeve, Christopher Reeve's adult children. Alexandra arrived early so that we would have a chance to talk before the party. She was only twenty-four at the time, and yet incredibly poised for her young age. She told me about finishing up her law degree at Columbia.

"What's your field?" I asked.

"Corporate law."

"And my field is lip balm," I deadpanned. She laughed. I think we both knew we'd get along. We talked about our hopes for the Champions Committee. The idea was to build support for the foundation from people age twenty-five to thirty-five. The committee was only in New York for the moment, but the idea was to expand it across the country as time went on. Later in the evening, I met Alexandra's brother, Matthew. He's a documentary filmmaker, and we spoke about the films he had made about his dad, including the TV special that I'd watched back in Mount Sinai.

Mr. Reeve had clearly inspired both of his children. Even though they weren't injured themselves, they had a real insight into what life is like for someone who is paralyzed. Matthew and Alexandra had both chosen to become the public faces of the organization after their father and stepmother passed away, and I admired them so much for that.

Only a handful of people knew it was my thirtieth birthday that evening. I wanted the focus to be on the Reeve Foundation and the need to raise money and awareness. I had a sense of the disparate pieces of my life converging to this one moment, and I was just so happy that the people I loved were there to see it.

28

Regeneration

TOWARD THE END OF 2008, WITH THE HOLIDAYS COMING around, I had one of my low periods. The holidays would often affect me in this way, reminding me that another year was passing, and that I was still in my chair. Even the most naturally happy person can't remain upbeat all of the time, and when you're dealing with an injury like this, it's an ongoing struggle to keep your spirits from sinking. There were days when I woke up and anticipated all the obstacles that lay ahead, wondering if I could get up the energy to go on. Everything seemed to be moving forward with the business and my involvement with the Reeve Foundation, but sometimes it felt as if I had bitten off more than I could chew. I was going to Burke-Cornell, doing my therapy, writing, developing Clark's Botanicals, working with the foundation. Maybe I was doing too much. The more I did, the more I wanted to do, and the more frustrated I became by the slow pace my injury continued to impose on me.

One night, my parents came home from their office after going through the day's paperwork as they usually did. I heard the car in the drive and it woke me up. I lay awake, waiting for my mom to come and see me, her nightly ritual before going to bed. That particular night, I caught a glimpse of her in the doorway as she was coming into my room. She paused there for a minute, and in that moment, I recognized as I often did, just how tired she looked. Both of my parents were in their sixties now, but there was no way they could think about retirement. They would have to keep working as long as they were able, in order to provide for me and to pay for all my expenses. In the nearly seven years since my accident, my mother rarely had more than a moment for herself.

"You OK?" I asked her.

"Of course, Francesco, just tired."

"Me too," I said. "Sometimes it feels like it's too much."

"You're doing a lot right now, Checco, but it's good. It's what you want. It keeps you going."

"I know," I said, agreeing with her. "But now that I have the creams, I can never switch off from work. It's always there, something I'm always dealing with."

Sometimes I would dream about just escaping everything and running away on vacation. It was December in New York, and every day seemed grayer and colder than the last. It would be so nice to go somewhere warm, but I knew that getting away was impossible. There was too much expense involved, and I needed too much equipment. We would have to take my standing frame so I could stand up, my Hoyer lift to get me into and out of bed, and my hospital bed that turned my body over in the night. And what kind of vacation would it be for my mother when she would need to look after me every minute of each day?

Even so, I wanted to indulge the fantasy for a moment.

"What if we could go away somewhere, for a vacation, like we used to?" I asked my mother. We had traveled to so many places as a family, but since I'd been injured, my parents had been home

with me continuously, never going away for more than a day or so
at a time. None of us had been on a proper vacation since my accident.

"We could go to Bermuda," my mother daydreamed. "Find
somewhere by the beach and just sleep."

"Do you remember the time we went to Florida, right before?"

"That was a long time ago now, Checco," said my mother wist-
fully.

"I want you to go on vacation," I told her. "I can't go, but that
doesn't mean you can't go. You and Dad could go together. You
deserve it. I want you to put me in assisted living for a week so
you can go away together. Please."

"No," my mother said adamantly. "Firstly, where is the money
coming from? And even if we had the money, why would we want
to go away without you? I wouldn't enjoy one minute. I won't hear
of it."

"But what kind of quality of life is this for you?" I wanted to
know. "How are you going to keep this up? I worry about you.
You have to do something for yourself."

"Francesco, you don't understand," she said, her tone rising
almost in anger. "I am your mother. This is the way it is, and this
is the way it's going to be. Everyone is given a different life. Everyone has to do different things. I have to do this, and it is not a
burden. Your father and I deal with what we have with a good
attitude. You're a gift to us, just like your brother and sister. This
is done. Nothing more to discuss. I am here with you."

I knew that I was no match for her resolve. If my injury has
done anything positive for me, then I would say it has increased
my ability for gratitude. In the past, like any young person, I've
been guilty of taking my parents for granted. Since my injury, I
knew exactly how fortunate I was to be their son. "OK, Mamma,"
I told her. "Thank you."

My mother checked that I was settled for the night ahead, that my catheter was changed, that my legs were straight, that I wasn't too hot, that my blankets were covering me. I wished her good night, and then she kissed me on my forehead and she was gone.

I knew I had to find a way of lifting myself out of this slump. I went back to my old trick of figuring out what came next to keep me from feeling down. At the beginning of the new year, I became involved in a new study at Burke-Cornell. The robotic-arm study was drawing to a close, and I was casting around for something else. Dr. Victor mentioned to me that his colleague, Dr. Everett, was working on a new study using repetitive trans-cranial magnetic stimulation (TMS) to help reactivate the par-alyzed muscles of stroke patients. I told Dr. Victor that I'd like to be considered for the study. Soon afterward, I met with Dr. Everett and he agreed to work with me. The study was exciting, but it also took a lot out of me physically. The TMS involved pulsing my brain with electrical stimulation repeatedly, a sensa-tion that was both uncomfortable and exhausting.

At the beginning of each session, a nylon mesh swim cap was pulled over my head with lines drawn on it so that the researchers could judge which part of the brain they were stimulating. (The cap also had the effect of making me look like a Cirque du Soleil acrobat who got lost on his way to the circus.) Dr. Everett's assis-tants placed electrodes on my arms so they could measure any muscular contractions as a result of the electrical pulses to the brain. They used certain electrodes to pulse muscles in my body, while pulsing my brain at the same time in order to further stim-ulate those areas. I would sit in my chair wearing my swim cap while one of the researchers began to press two large magnetic coils to the front of my scalp.

The first time I did this, I was a little apprehensive. "Wait a minute," I stalled. "Is this going to hurt?"

"Oh, no," they told me. "It doesn't hurt. You may sense a pulling sensation under your scalp, and various muscles may twitch."

Then they squeezed the coil against my head and clicked. The charge surged through my being. My entire brain jolted inside my head.

"*Aoww!*" I wailed, flailing my arm and accidentally hitting my doctor. "That *really* hurt." It was the strangest sensation, something you definitely didn't want to experience a second time around—like a giant rubber band snapping inside your head. All I could think was, *Please* don't do that again. In fact, they would have to pulse my brain 120 times every visit. With each click, my shoulders would inch closer and closer to my ears. When they'd finished, my body would be so tense from the pulsing that it was very hard for me to wind down. The first time I got zapped, I felt cold for twelve hours; I couldn't warm up. I was ghostly pale and had an intense headache. My jaw didn't unclench until the following day.

Over time, I became more tolerant of the treatment, although I'd be lying if I said I enjoyed it. Even so, I was sensing that the treatment was worthwhile. One day in early March, Dr. Everett came to speak with me after I finished my session. He had good news for me. He was starting to see responses in muscles that I wasn't supposed to be able to use. I was reacting to the brain shocks in my wrist flexors, my triceps, even in some of my finger muscles.

"What is happening is that we're seeing a definite connection between parts of your brain and parts of your body that have been paralyzed for years," Dr. Everett explained.

This was more proof for me that my spinal cord was finding a way of regenerating itself. I knew for a fact that my arms had become more relaxed as a result of the TMS. Before, I could straighten them, but the motion was always jerky, never smooth.

Now when I straightened my arms, it looked natural, as if I'd always done it this way.

"We don't exactly know why this is happening," Dr. Everett told me. "You're one of the first spinal-cord-injury patients to try this. But it seems the TMS is uncovering that your body is adjusting, overcoming the block created by the initial spinal-cord damage, and slowly allowing some function."

When I got home, there was more good news waiting for me. The new president, Barack Obama, had signed an executive order lifting the restrictions on federal funding of human embryonic stem-cell research. My family and I had been on tenterhooks since the inauguration, waiting to hear when he was going to lift the ban. "When's he going to do it?" my mother would ask me on a daily basis. In his announcement, Obama spoke about leaving behind the "false choice between sound science and moral values." He went on to talk about support for scientists who pursue this kind of research: "We will aim for America to lead the world in the discoveries it one day may yield."

My phone was buzzing with e-mails and calls that day. *Did you hear? Are you excited?* "Yes, I'm excited," I would reply. For the entirety of my paralysis there had been this restriction on science, and now scientists could go on with their work. Obviously this was great news. But now that the new order was finally here, I felt elation mixed with disappointment. Part of me felt like the Wright Brothers had built the plane, but nobody knew how to fly it. We had lost eight years. So much damage has been done, not just to science, but also to people's perceptions of the whole stem-cell debate. When Bush announced his ruling in 2001, he did so while standing next to forty parents holding in-vitro babies. It was a deliberately provocative photo-op, turning stem cells into a hot-button, politicized subject. By contrast, when Obama repealed Bush's decision, it felt like a three-second blip on TV.

Meanwhile, I wanted a ticker-tape parade in Manhattan, at the very least. So many people had worked so hard for that blink of an eye, but now we found ourselves faced with a new challenge. In many ways, this felt even harder. We had to plan for what was going to come next. We needed to expand our horizons and push for a cure, but with more urgency and intelligence than ever before.

EPILOGUE

Here Today

"NOW START TO PUSH WITH YOUR ARMS AND LEGS SO THAT you're moving forward," my trainer tells me.

I'm down on my knees, propped on my elbows, and my trainer is holding my hips. He's guiding me, but the rest I'm doing myself. I'm crawling forward on my elbows. Then I crawl backwards. In the same way that babies have to build the necessary muscles for walking by crawling, I'm using every muscle available to me—in my abs, my back, my triceps, my shoulders, my pecs—to move around on all fours. To do this, I need my trainer to hold my hips, but I can also do a modified version alone, lying flat on my belly and moving my body around by using my elbows. After we finish up, my body aches from the intensity of the workout. The more sensation I recover, the more it hurts. Just this past week, I started to feel the muscles in my back. As I sit here writing this, my back is achy and sore—my triceps and shoulders, too. The irony is that the more function I regain, the more therapy I have to do to help alleviate the pain. Even so, I'll always take pain over nothing at all.

It's springtime 2009. Through the window of my bedroom, I can see the flowers bloom on the patio. My mom's outside gardening. All is peaceful in suburbia. Even so, this is a time of year that brings back the past. Whenever it's the first sunny day of spring, I know the anniversary of my accident is coming around, and the flashbacks will soon begin. In the night I wake from dreams that are so real I think it's seven years ago, and I've just been injured. I can taste, feel, and smell the chlorine water. I'm scared of the nurse coming into the room to suction my lungs. I wake up gasping for air because my body doesn't think that it can breathe. When I do wake up, I have to remind myself that I'm alive and that I continue to get better, bit by bit.

For a long time, I couldn't imagine my future. All I wanted to do was turn back the clock, to live in the past, to return to my life as it was before. Slowly, very slowly, I began to look for alternatives to the traditional models of treatment, and even more slowly, I started to see results. Physical therapy became my life, and getting better became my obsession. Everything else was put on hold until I could walk again. As the years passed, I realized that I was actually limiting myself by thinking in this way. These days, I'm still working on getting better, but I'm finding ways to live my life at the same time. I don't want to get to the point where I can finally walk, only to look around and realize that I forgot to enjoy myself in the process.

I believe that I do have a full life. I'm working on my business. I'm doing therapy each day. I'm contributing to the work of the Reeve Foundation; I continue to participate in research studies at Burke-Cornell. And I'm having a good time. Walking is not my end goal; it's not my reason for living, because I feel as if it's inevitable that I *will* walk. My expectation is that there will be a cure in the next five years. I don't say this out of naiveté; I'm a doctor's son. I'm basing my expectation on scientific reality. I'm doing my research. I'm involved in the process. At the time of my writing this, the researchers at the Miami Project to Cure Paralysis in Florida plan to begin human clinical trials in 2010, using the same type of stem cells they've previously used successfully on mice, right here in the United States. Many researchers around the world are actively showing that promoting nerve regrowth and regeneration is possible. For so long, it was assumed that paralysis after a spinal-cord injury was irreversible. That assumption is hard to defend anymore. What I've learned since my accident is that whether you're disabled or able-bodied, you cannot define yourself by the expectations of others. When I was told after my injury that I would never breathe without a ventilator again or move from my bed, I could have accepted that diagnosis. Instead, together with my family, we decided to go beyond that limited vision. Scientists, researchers, funders, doctors, patients, politicians—we all need to go beyond our preconceived notions of what's possible if we want to move ahead. But while I wait to hear about the next step in science, my personal goal is to live a happy life and to contribute to society.

I have many hopes for the future. Clark's Botanicals is becoming a bigger company, and I want to continue to help it to grow. We're winning awards. We've been taken on by Saks Fifth Avenue department store in New York. We're now sold in Italy, Korea, Japan, and China. As the company expands, I find that my longing to have my independence back becomes even greater. I would love to live alone again, and this is something that still feels so far beyond my grasp. I know it's going to happen, but I have to become physically independent, and I also need to become financially independent before I can get to that point. In the same way that I don't rule out living alone, I would never shut myself off from the possibility of being in a relationship someday. But right now I'm at the stage of my life where I'm very focused on my work and my recovery. Who knows what the future will bring? This much I've learned from my injury: If something's going to happen to you, it's going to happen. I can only do my best, and that means carrying on. I have a close family, good friends, and I am surrounded by love, which I think helps me enormously.

In many ways, it's the little things that get to me, not the bigger-picture questions. There are those times when I just want to walk to a theater and go to a movie, and I can't, and that gets to me. Right now, it would be nice to get up and make myself a cup of coffee. Last week I had a meeting in the city and my friend couldn't drive me at the last minute, so I couldn't go. Without a doubt, there are days when I feel demoralized. Why is it that I can't just get up in the morning and jump in the shower? Why does going to the bathroom have to be such a big deal? Why does going out for dinner have to be such a production? Why can't I just go somewhere on my own? The more I achieve with the business and with my life, the more the injury seems to get in my way. It's not as if all this ceases to bother me. In fact, sometimes it bothers me more than it used to, because I'm so much busier now.

In all of this, my family continues to provide me with an unimaginable level of care and support. Despite the sacrifices they've made and continue to make, I'm happy to say that since the time of my injury, our family continues to grow. My sister has graduated medical school and is getting married this spring to a man she met while studying medicine. My brother and his wife have started a family. They have a three-year-old, Orsino, and a baby, Brigitte. Our numbers are multiplying, and our sense of what our family means has expanded. My parents are besotted with their grandchildren. They're delighted that my sister has graduated and is settling down, that my brother has found his niche and has this wonderful new family. They're happy that despite my injury, I'm thriving. They continue to work hard, and must do so, in large part because of the enormous cost of my living expenses. Every day, I wake up with an inherent sense of guilt because I need them so completely. But by making something of my life, by getting out of that bed each morning and going on, I feel as if I can pay them back in some small way for everything they've done for me.

I continue to be a very proud uncle. Two years ago, my little nephew Orsino learned to stand up by pushing himself up on my wheelchair. Today, he thinks that the ramp on our van is the coolest thing he's ever seen. He stands there agape as I descend on my lift. He's three now, and when he comes to visit, the first word out of his mouth as he runs down the drive is: "Checco!" When I've finished my work or my therapy, we head outside and my brother puts him on my lap in the motorized wheelchair so we can take a spin down the street.

"Faster! Faster!" Orsino shrieks, wriggling and laughing in my lap.

I push the button on my chair, all the way up to full speed, and we just go.

ACKNOWLEDGMENTS

WRITING THIS BOOK WAS AN INCREDIBLE EXPERIENCE FOR me. It forced me to relive the darkest moment of my life in such detail and in so many different dimensions that at times, I wanted to throw my hands up in the air and give up. Then, something shifted. As I revisited each phase of my life since my injury, I was reminded just how lucky I am to have my incredible family and friends, who don't see a wheelchair, or four wheels, and who won't tolerate any sort of excuse.

So many people helped me with this book. Carol Mann, my agent, my cheerleader, who believed in me since the day we met, and gently nudged me to push harder. Eve Charles, who helped me flesh out my emotions on paper when I felt I couldn't delve deeper into myself. Leslie Wells, my lovely editor, who is also a delight to have as a friend. Hyperion Books, because they really stepped up to the plate for me.

Mary Alice Stephenson, who loves me so much and supports me so much that it stupefies me. Glenda Bailey, for making me laugh and giving me advice on Clark's Botanicals, life, and some delightful fashion. Kerry Diamond, because her heart is so big and her soul so generous, I still have no idea how to show her I love her just as much. Amanda Ross, who got me a spot at Mount Sinai in two days flat. Kim-Van Dang, for seeing my kooky idea for a company and helping it soar. Jeanine Lobell, for being the tough, Balenciaga-clad bodyguard in the background. Linda Wells, who replies to my off-the-wall e-mails with a "call me now." Jane Larkworthy, because she is not only an amazing friend, but also took a risk on Clark's Botanicals and me. Robin Coe Hutshing, because she let me talk her ear off and believed in my vision. Costello Tagliapietra, for listening, talking, and friendship. Elisa Lipsky-Karasz, who supports me completely no matter how crazy I may be. Grace Alonso, who constantly surprises me with her generosity and humor. Victoria Kirby and Jennifer Meyer because they don't let me stop, ever. Patricia Margro, who loves me unconditionally, and I still don't know why. Maggie Goldberg, for always doing more. Heather Duchowny and Matthew Snyder, because they saw me as a person, not a client.

Peter Wilderotter, who is the coolest, most supportive friend ever. Peter Kiernan, for his complete dedication to the Reeve Foundation and for his friendship. Aimee Hunnewell, because she sticks up for me and anyone with a disability, and keeps me motivated with her fun, spunky energy. Patricia Stush, for believing in me. Alexandra Reeve Givens, because she's a true friend, supportive, and keeps her father's dream a reality. Matthew Reeve, for his calm, stoic leadership for the Reeve Foundation and for his friendship.

Andrew Klein, the best physical therapist on this planet, but with really bad, horrible jokes. Maldon, because his jokes are actually funny. Dr. Ursula Jacob, for helping me move my abs and back again. Eliza Kane, Laura Santucci, Darryl Hendricks, Kathryn Whitney, Julia Murphy, Caitlin King, and Lucy Gwathmy for showing up every day and forcing me to move, even when I didn't want to. Dr. Dothlyn Dennis, my good friend, for being there, always. Geri Richter Campbell, for constantly challenging me. The doctors and researchers at the Kessler Foundation Research Center, for working with me on the treadmill study. Everyone at Burke-Cornell for zapping my brain, hooking me up to robots, and helping my recovery. All of my doctors, nurses, and personal aides, because they keep my body healthy. All of the great therapists at the Rehabilitation Institute of Michigan in Detroit who made me move my legs.

Dr. Ellen Carney, my former high school teacher and now friend, because she can make me see the smile in anything. Fiorella Saponara, Eleanor Chung, Alex Lunney, Colleen Bramhall, Beth Mullin, Katie Seymour, Dana Sindona, Jessica Christian, for supporting me, helping me, and being the best friends ever. Dagmar Fisher, Beth McFadden, Dina Thakarar, Laura Santos, Mara Sombrotto, Amanda Davis, Erika Albies, Alexis Weiss, Natasha Royt, Rebecca Guinness, Karen Marsala, Amy Cording, Tara Hanson, Malika Gandhi, for making me laugh and showing me I'll never be alone. Therese and Frank Szigethy, for your love, support, and prayers—and pizza. Vincent Lentini, for your generous and kind heart. Suzan Colon, for everything; I am lucky to be your friend.

My incredible parents, Dr. Mariella S. Clark and Dr. Harold Chandler Clark, for their love, unstoppable spirit, and creative solutions to life's sometimes seemingly impossible bumps. Nonna Trippi, *perche' sei bravissima e sei fatta d'oro*. My amazing brother, Harold Michael Clark, for surprising everyone with his calm, leading presence. Valerie Clark, for keeping my brother in check and being an all-around great person. Charlotte Clark Avedissian, for being the most caring and coolest sister ever. Manuel Avedissian, for joining our crazy family and for being such a grounding presence within it. Orsino Clark, because he's going to grow up to be a great guy, even though he already is. Brigitte Clark, for her undeniable caring soul, even at two years old.

I'm sure I'm forgetting so many others. If I have, I'll take you out to dinner to make up for it.

DATE DUE
